Italian Pure and Simple

Italian
Pure and Simple

ROBUST AND RUSTIC HOME COOKING
FOR EVERY DAY

Clifford A. Wright

WILLIAM MORROW AND COMPANY, INC., NEW YORK

Library of Congress Cataloging-in-Publication Data

Wright, Clifford A.
Italian pure and simple / Clifford A. Wright.—1st ed.
p.   cm.
Includes index.
ISBN 0-688-15306-2
1. Cookery, Italian.   I. Title.
TX723.W752 1998
641.5945—dc21   97-14728
CIP

Printed in the United States of America

First Edition

1 2 3 4 5 6 7 8 9 10

BOOK DESIGN BY OKSANA KUSHNIR

www.williammorrow.com

This book is dedicated
to my father, Harold I. Wright,
and my mother, Helen De Yeso Wright,
because they gave me
such a wonderful and fun childhood.

ACKNOWLEDGMENTS

The cooking that happens in my home is Italian pure and simple. It is robust food that I cook for the everyday eating of my kids and friends. It's my home cooking. Hence the simple title of this book. The best preparations in my mom's repertoire are Italian foods that she learned by virtue of being part Italian. I remember well those soulful dinners of spaghetti and meat balls or baked rigatoni. So to write a cookbook about robust family-style Italian cooking there was no better way than to share the experience with my three kids, Ali, Dyala, and Seri, with their adventurous palates, and all my friends and their children. Because I'm divorced and my dad, mom, and sister are scattered to the four corners of this country, a story familiar to many American families, I want to thank my friends for letting me experiment on them both as quasi-family members and as recipe test tasters, and for letting me make a shambles of their kitchens in the hope that the family-style meal being prepared was worth it all. Thanks to Mark Chalek, Jenny Lavigne, Harry Irwin, Pam Haltom, David Forbes, Ginny Sherwood, Nancy Lang, Marsha and Bob Sanders, Eric Stange, Barbara Costa, and all their children for sharing the food and good times.

I also want to thank my agent, Doe Coover, and my editor, Pam Hoenig, both of whom have faith in my rather varied projects. Without their support and wise suggestions none of these efforts could be realized.

CONTENTS

How to Cook Simple, Robust, Family-Style Italian Food

My memory of it is dimming. It was a bright and sunny June day and my grandfather's brothers and their extended families were driving down from Massachusetts to Long Island; it was going to be my first time meeting them. I remember the trunk of their car opening and seeing in it piles of homemade macaroni packed in bags. My aunt and uncle had set up a long table on their patio, and we ate and ate and talked and talked, and laughed. There were at least twenty people, relatives all. And it went on all day, it seemed. We drank Chianti and ate macaroni with as luscious a ragù as I've ever had. My grandfather Raphael De Yeso died soon after, and I realized later that his brothers had come to say their good-byes.

My grandfather cooked the dishes he ate as a boy growing

up in a little village near Benevento—robust, rustic foods from the old country. But his four children were Americanized and, except for an occasional dish that reflected their heritage, they cooked American food. All I knew was that the food we had that day was extraordinary, and I wanted to eat like that always, and have my children eat like that always. So we do. And this book will let you cook the kind of Italian-inspired food that will make your family happy.

Italian food has captured the American imagination. *Ristoranti, trattorias,* and brick-oven pizzerias now dot the landscape from coast to coast. Yet most families would consider cooking an authentic, delicious Italian meal at home on short notice an impossibility. Your average workday mom and dad come home tired, the kids are wild and hungry, and the all-too-often solution is (bad) take-out pizza. Now and then this quick fix suffices, but in our hearts we know that a robust and savory home-cooked meal is a far better and healthier alternative to the overcheesed, soggy-crusted dreck they call pizza in most parlors. Who could resist a steaming platter of garlicky tomato sauce covering pork chops and Italian sausages and the aroma of crusty bread dipped in olive oil, accompanied by a glass of Chianti and a side dish of baby spinach leaves with olive oil and garlic? Sound like too much trouble for a middle-of-the-week menu? Not by a long shot. With a well-stocked pantry and a little planning, this fabulous dinner can be on the table in about half an hour.

Italian Pure and Simple is full of the robust and rustic recipes that satisfy hungry families. These easy recipes are reminiscent of the meals I ate with my relatives or at various *trattorias* in Italy, and of course my mother's Italian cooking, like her baked rigatoni, a family favorite. These Italian family recipes are easy to follow, flexible, nutritionally balanced, quick, and have great taste—robust, delicious Italian flavors that will excite the palate and solve the Monday-to-Friday dilemma.

Feeding families often means keeping it simple. Many of these recipes are one-platter meals—what the Italians calls *piatti unici*. The cook will relish the ease of putting rigatoni with fried yellow and red bell peppers on the table, while the family will love the powerful aroma of garlic, fennel seeds, and oregano that wafts from the kitchen on a cold winter night. Another cold-weather favorite in my family is penne with roasted chestnuts and grilled sausage. There's nothing quite like the smell of roasted chestnuts in the house when you come back inside from turning sausages that are sizzling on the grill (increasingly, grill aficionados have made it a year-round activity).

Pasta, as the Italians know, is the perfect foundation for meat, vegetables, fish, sauces, and even fruit and nuts. A tantalizing meal of fettuccine with rib eye steak and sautéed spinach seasoned with garlic and cayenne pepper is a cinch to prepare and will have everyone asking for seconds. Simpler still, and a real "*trattoria* treat," is fettuccine tossed with boneless veal and artichoke hearts in a sauce of reduced wine and parsley—a great late-night dinner. On a brisk autumn day, my children loved to eat capellini with ground lamb and chopped tomatoes cooked with Chianti wine.

The bulk of the recipes in *Italian Pure and Simple* are flavorful pasta dishes, but there are many recipes for lighter dinners. Dark, earthy-tasting portabella mushrooms tossed with fresh parsley and freshly grated Parmesan (Parmigiano-Reggiano) cheese, and whipped with eggs and olive oil, make a satisfying frittata. And few fish can top a belly cut of fresh bluefin tuna drizzled with olive oil, grilled over a hot fire, and covered with a *salsa verde* of parsley and garlic. I also hope to introduce you to preparations that use less expensive, but equally good-tasting fish, such as a pan-fried ocean pout (also called ling) with chives, which can become your family's "poor man's lobster" dinner. In addition, the desserts are healthy fruit-based recipes, such as mangoes in lime syrup, a heavenly concoction of ripe mangoes covered with a syrupy sauce of lime and mint leaves.

Italian families care about the food they eat. They pay attention to quality so they can eat gloriously fresh green vegetables cooked to retain their natural sweetness. Only the plumpest, vine-ripened tomatoes are used in their sauces. Their basil, oregano, and other fresh herbs are picked just before cooking. The fish comes right out of the sea, hours old, and they use red meat in smaller portions too, along with other aromatic ingredients, adding flavor without excess fat.

Planning and cooking Italian-inspired foods for your family is easier with an appropriately stocked refrigerator and pantry. My recipes assume that essential ingredients will be on hand. I'll be asking you to think Italian, act Italian, and cook Italian. Remember that without garlic cloves, extra-virgin olive oil, succulent olives, capers, golden raisins, pine nuts, Parmesan cheese in large chunks, fresh mozzarella, and boxes of different dried pastas, it will be impossible to keep dinner simple, let alone Italian style. It's also helpful to know a local Italian market (every city has at least one) where you can find a variety of salamis, imported prosciutto, roasted red peppers, Italian cheeses, salted anchovies, and all the other products that make Italian food so deliciously unique. To find them look in the Yellow Pages under "Italian Food Products" or "Markets" or "Grocers—Retail." You could also call an Italian restaurant and ask the chef or manager where to buy Italian food products.

Fortunately, many supermarkets already carry these Italian food staples. My mother, who lives in a gastronomically challenged area of west-central Florida, always complains that her friends (who love Italian food) can't find the "exotic" foods, as she calls them, that I allegedly call for in the recipes, such as pine nuts and pancetta. Finally, I got tired of the complaints and decided to drag her to the local Winn-Dixie, convinced that we would find both those ingredients there. Sure enough, the pine nuts were on the shelf and the pancetta was at the deli counter, admittedly a little hard to find. So I turned to my mom and said, "You and your friends are just lazy; you don't want to look, to make the effort." She laughed, knowing this to be true—it's something about retired life. But if you want good Italian food, you can't be lazy, you've got to make some effort. But "effort" doesn't mean back-breaking work, just simple caring—caring enough to put the best meal possible on the table for your family and friends. The greatest reward for any cook is to see empty plates and a happy family. When my ex-wife calls me up for the recipe to the spinach dish that our three kids are raving about, that's satisfaction (it's on page 234).

When most people think of an Italian family, they have in mind a stereotypical Italian-American family from a big East Coast city, with "mama" in the kitchen and at least eight people sitting at a table crowded and raucous with *spezzatini, braciole,* and macaroni with ragù. So your family isn't around for you to share the table? Sure they are. This is the turn of the millennium, where the concept of family means your kids, your friends, and their kids. Oh, your family never eats together? Well, insist on it: light a candle next time, make a delicious Lasagnette with Pancetta and White Onions (page 81), and rather than ask the kids how school was, make some totally outrageous statement and get everyone arguing over dinner. All of sudden no one is bored, they're not leaving the table, and they're noticing how good dinner was.

The authentic tastes of Italy *can* be captured in the American kitchen. Family-style Italian food is based on two "secrets": freshness and simplicity. What does "family-style" mean? First, of course, it means meals that families eat together. For the cook it means recipes that are easy to follow, are quick, taste great, provide nutritional balance, and disappear in a flash because the family loves this kind of food. I can't tell you how often my family has smelled an enticing aroma coming from the kitchen and rushed in to see what's cooking, only to find that all I've done so far is sauté some onions and garlic in extra-virgin olive oil. It's that simple.

Some years ago I wrote a book called *Cucina Rapida* (William Morrow, 1994), with recipes and explanations on how you could cook fast Italian-inspired meals in minutes with all those great tastes you remember from your sojourns in Italy, or that you tasted at some quaint *trattoria* in New York, Chicago, or San Francisco. In this book I pay attention to time—the recipes don't really take long to cook—but I'm more concerned with your need for recipes to taste good and be easy. Here "easy" means cooking in the Italian style where the emphasis is on simple, fresh cooking. In fact, fresh vegetables, besides tasting better, are easier than frozen vegetables because you don't defrost them.

I know these recipes will please your palate, meet your concern for time, and push you toward an inspired Italian-style cookery. You will find a large number of pasta recipes. I love pasta because it is delicious, nutritious, and the perfect foundation for vegetables, meat, fish, sauces, and even fruit, as you will see in several recipes. Italians eat pasta as a *primo piatto,* or first course, to be followed by a second course of meat or fish. In deference to our American lifestyle, and with apologies to purists, the pasta recipes in my book can also be *piatti unici*—that is, one-platter meals to be served as a meal, perhaps with a vegetable on the side or whatever else you prefer. But I will occasionally serve dinner to my family in three courses, usually on a weekend night. I don't do it often, but when I do, my kids think it's "cool."

To capture those authentic tastes of Italy in your kitchen in the shortest possible time and be most pleasing to the people for whom you are cooking, remember these "secrets" (if they can be called that):

1. Care about the food. When shopping for food, pay attention to quality: look, smell, touch, and, if you can, taste the food. Don't settle for any stalk of broccoli; get the one that is bright green with tightly packed florets. Stay away from processed foods except the ones mentioned in this book. Visit your local farmer's markets.

2. Buy for "freshness," not price. This goes for vegetables and fish especially. Old vegetables and old fish might be cheap, but you pay the price at the table: no one eats it.

3. Make sure that the contents of your pantry and refrigerator make sense for Italian cooking. Does your dry pantry have olive oil, spaghetti, tomato puree, garlic, capers, salted anchovies, and red and white wine vinegars? Does your spice cabinet have crumbled dried oregano leaf? Does your refrigerator have olives, pine nuts, pancetta, and Parmesan and Pecorino cheese? Remember that Italians don't use lemongrass on their pasta nor pineapple on their pizza.

4. Seek out an Italian market. There are Italian markets all over the United States. A little experiment I conduct when I visit friends and family around the country is to find that Italian market in their town. Of course, this is no problem in big cities such as New York, San Francisco, Chicago, or Boston. But there are so many people of Italian heritage in this country that finding the food stores they have opened up really shouldn't be hard.

Although I emphasize freshness, the recipes here are flexible enough so the cook can use some processed food products that will not harm the overall taste, such as canned artichoke hearts in water, cooked chick-peas, and canned tomato products such as whole plum tomatoes, tomato puree, and tomato paste. There are a few frozen vegetables that can also be satisfactory, but I limit these to artichoke hearts, peas, and lima beans. Notice that I used the word *satisfactory*, not *preferred*. I do not prefer frozen products, but sometimes they are perfect when you are in a pinch for time and don't want to peel five pounds of pea pods.

The recipes in *Italian Pure and Simple* are all new recipes in the sense that they are all Italian inspired, but not so familiar that we've seen them a thousand times. And they are flexible enough to allow the cook to plan dinner either as a pasta-based one-platter meal (a *piatto unico*), perhaps with a salad, or as a more relaxed meal with a first course (*primo piatto*) and a second course (*secondo piatto*) of meat, chicken, or fish with an accompanying vegetable dish.

Now go to it. Have fun, and remember that this is not brain surgery but cooking. One more thing—taste the food as you cook; that's the only way to know if you're getting it right.

Italian Pure and Simple

CHAPTER ONE

Antipasti, Crostini, and Other Little Foods

When I was growing up, antipasto meant a platter of iceberg lettuce, a couple of rolled-up pieces of salami, slices of domestic provolone cheese, and a few olives. After traveling to Italy many times over the past thirty years, however, I was introduced to what antipasti really means: everything from a few sticks of carrot or broccoli stalks dipped in a bagna cauda, to involved preparations that could be considered dinner themselves. I love antipasti and other little foods from Italy, such as panini, crostini, or pizzette. For the family I serve any of these little foods well before dinner. I can keep the kids satisfied, and these treats certainly stimulate the appetite. Best of all, they are a great way to get kids to eat vegetables that they might not otherwise try. And adults love the earthy taste of preparations like Veal Marrow Crostini (page 12).

Anchovy and Parsley Butter

Make this aromatic butter ahead of time; keep it refrigerated and you will have a great seasoning for pasta when you need one in a jiffy.

MAKES ABOUT $1/2$ CUP

———

1/2 cup (1 stick) unsalted butter, at room temperature
1/4 cup very finely chopped fresh parsley leaves
8 salted anchovy fillets, rinsed and patted dry
2 garlic cloves, very finely chopped
2 teaspoons freshly squeezed lemon juice
Freshly ground black pepper to taste

———

1. In a mixing bowl, mash all the ingredients together with a fork until well blended.

2. Transfer to a sheet of aluminum foil or waxed paper, fold one end over it, and roll back and forth until it forms a cylinder. Twist the ends and refrigerate until needed; it will keep for up to 4 weeks.

If one could ask what the secret ingredient is to good Italian cooking, the answer would be anchovies. These are small silvery fish with a high fat content relative to other fish and a delicate, unsalty taste when eaten fresh, as they are in Italy. Anchovies are sold in four ways: fresh or frozen (although hard to find); as a paste sold in tubes; salted and packed in oil, sold in tiny cans layered flat or rolled, sometimes with a caper; and whole, packed in salt. The best are these whole salted anchovies sold in 1-pound cans or in bulk, bought from an Italian market. They will still have a little of their silver skin on. To prepare them, wash the salt off under running water, then separate the two fillets by opening up the slit belly. Rinse and peel the fillets off the bone.

This is the name of two different kinds of cheese. The first is the one used in this book, a dried cow's milk ricotta cheese. The ricotta curd is placed in a basket or perforated container and the water is pressed out. Then the ricotta is dried at a warm temperature. When it is sold, the younger version is called soft or eating ricotta salata, while the drier version is known as grating ricotta.

The second type of ricotta salata, which you are unlikely to come across in this country, is a sheep's milk cheese similar to Pecorino.

∾

Antipasto

When I walk into an Italian deli I'm transported to heaven on the distinctive aroma of suspended salamis, garlands of garlic, barrels of olives, and bowls filled with freshly made cheeses. But all too often many of us are at a loss in an Italian market. Well, this recipe is a list of what to get. You can use these ingredients to construct a spectacular antipasto to serve with fresh crusty Italian country bread.

In Italy there are hundreds of antipasti. This presentation is my high-quality version of the typical Italian-American antipasto that I grew up with. The porchetta (pronounced *pork-ETTA*) is an Italian roast pork available in Italian markets. Substitute any roast pork cold cut. Coppa is a cured ham, slightly more maroon in color than prosciutto and earthier. It is made of equal parts lean and fatty pig's shoulder seasoned with salt, pepper, and nutmeg for three months.

MAKES 6 SERVINGS

———

1 cup 1-inch green bean pieces
1 yellow bell pepper, roasted (page 68) and sliced into strips
2 red bell peppers, roasted (page 68) and sliced into strips
1 cup imported green olives
1 cup imported black olives
6 tablespoons extra-virgin olive oil
$1/4$ pound porchetta (Italian roast pork), sliced
$1/4$ pound prosciutto di Parma, sliced
$1/4$ pound Genoa salami, sliced
$1/4$ pound soppresatta, sliced
$1/4$ pound coppa, sliced
2 ounces mascarpone cheese

2 ounces Gorgonzola cheese
2 ounces ricotta salata cheese
2 ounces fresh mozzarella cheese, diced
Several slices crusty Italian or French bread

———

1. Bring a saucepan filled with water to a boil and blanch the green beans for 2 minutes. Remove and plunge in cold water to stop their cooking. Return the beans to boiling water and cook until tender.

2. On a large, round serving platter, place the yellow pepper strips in the center. Surround with the green beans. Surround the beans with the red peppers. On one side of the red peppers, place the green olives, and on the other, the black olives. Drizzle the olive oil over all of it.

3. Place the remaining ingredients, including the cheeses, around the edge of the platter, rolling or folding the cold cuts if you must. Break a piece of bread, dip it in some olive oil, and nibble an interchange of ingredients.

The only kind of table olives I find acceptable for good Italian cooking and eating are imported olives, usually sold loose in barrels of brine. Canned olives don't cut it because they are cured with lye, which renders the olive tasteless. Italian, Greek, and Middle Eastern markets are the best sources for olives. Often they will sell many varieties, both black and green. Among the Italian olives you might find are Gaeta, Paterno, or Cerignola. One olive is not better than another—it's just a matter of your taste.

∾

Ricotta Salata and Black Olives in Olive Oil

Black olives, white cheese. Splashed with olive oil, the glistening contrast of color is very appetizing. This preparation is nice served among other antipasti.

MAKES 2 SERVINGS

———

¹/₄ pound ricotta salata cheese, diced
12 small imported black olives
3 tablespoons extra-virgin olive oil

———

1. Mix all the ingredients together very carefully.

2. Serve on a flat plate with crusty Italian bread.

Involtini di Lattuga
(Lettuce Cigars)

Lettuce roll-ups stuffed with a crab and ricotta pâté is a great party snack or appetizer, and the leftovers make a nice frittata.

MAKES 4 SERVINGS

———

1/2 pound cooked crabmeat, picked over for shells and cartilage
6 ounces ricotta cheese
1/2 cup freshly grated mild provolone or Parmesan cheese
1/2 cup mayonnaise, or to taste
Salt and freshly ground black pepper to taste
Cayenne pepper to taste
Romaine lettuce leaves, central ribs removed

———

1. In a medium bowl, mix the crabmeat, cheeses, and mayonnaise. Season with salt, pepper, and cayenne.

2. Put a tablespoon of crab mixture in a portion of lettuce leaf and roll up. Arrange on a platter and serve.

RICOTTA

~

Ricotta, which means "recooked," is a by-product of provolone cheese making. Because it is an uncured cheese, use only the fresh ricotta found in Italian markets and in better quality supermarkets. Commercially made ricotta is satisfactory as a substitute, although it does contain preservatives.

Italian ricotta is made from whey coagulated with an acid such as vinegar or lemon juice. That is not always the case in this country, where skim milk is sometimes added. When it is fresh, ricotta cheese has an amazing taste—creamy, yet intriguingly bland.

~

One could write a book on olive oil. Rather than do that, let me suggest what should be in your pantry in the way of olive oil. Keep three kinds of olive oil handy. The first should be a high-quality, cold-pressed, estate-bottled extra-virgin olive oil with its distinctively personal taste, to be used sparingly with uncooked dishes or for drizzling on finished cooked dishes; this olive oil should never be heated. The second should be a good-quality but inexpensive commercial extra-virgin olive oil or a good-quality olive oil called simply "olive oil" (and sometimes "virgin" or "pure") for cooking at low to medium-high temperatures.

The third oil should be an inexpensive olive oil, olive oil blend, or olive pomace oil for any cooking calling for very hot oil. Olive pomace oil is

Ricotta and Hazelnut Fritters

A last-minute antipasto. This is a great little preparation to slap together for a snack or appetizer.

MAKES 16 FRITTERS

———

1 cup all-purpose flour or leftover mashed potatoes
3/4 cup ricotta cheese
1/4 cup chopped hazelnuts
Salt to taste
1/8 teaspoon ground cinnamon
Dry bread crumbs for dredging
6 cups olive oil for frying

———

1. Mix the flour or mashed potatoes with the ricotta, hazelnuts, salt, and cinnamon. Form into croquettes (about the size of a man's thumb) and dredge in the bread crumbs, tapping off any excess. Set aside.

2. Preheat the frying oil in a deep fryer to 360°F or in an 8-inch saucepan over medium-high heat until almost smoking, about 10 minutes. Fry the croquettes (don't crowd the pan; you'll have to fry them in several batches) until golden brown, 4 to 5 minutes, turning occasionally.

3. Drain on paper towels and serve immediately. Let the frying oil cool, then strain and save.

Roasted Country Bread with Ricotta

I often make this for a weekend breakfast when I want something a little different. It's ideal with a cup of coffee or a glass of freshly squeezed orange juice.

MAKES 4 SERVINGS

————

4 large ³/₄-inch-thick slices Italian or French round country bread,
cut from the center
1 pound ricotta cheese, preferably fresh
Extra-virgin olive oil for drizzling
Salt and freshly ground black pepper to taste

————

1. Preheat the oven to 400°F.

2. Coat the slices of bread with the ricotta cheese and place on a baking sheet. Drizzle some olive oil over them and season with salt and pepper. Place in the oven until the oil starts bubbling, about 10 minutes.

the oil made from the pits and pulp of the olives. It is inexpensive and ideal for deep-frying.

Red pepper oil can be made by placing ten to twenty dried red chili peppers in a bottle of extra-virgin olive oil and leaving it for two weeks before using. It is best not to make other kinds of flavored oils at home because of the danger of bacterial contamination, so leave that to the professionals.

~

Caciocavallo is a hard spun-curd cheese made from cow's milk. A spun-curd cheese, or *pasta filata,* is so called because the drained curd is soaked in hot whey, then in water, and finally stretched, molded, and spun by the cheese maker. Among these stringlike cheeses are mozzarella, provolone, and scamorze. Caciocavallo is hung in the form of two gourds tied together. The outside is a smooth pale yellow while the inside is nearly white. The cheese itself is very dense.

Caciocavallo, of which there are many varieties, is mostly made in southern Italy and Sicily. It can be eaten plain (when younger) and grated (when older). Caciocavallo is almost exclusively found in Italian markets. Imported provolone is an excellent substitute.

~

Fried Caciocavallo

This is ridiculously simple to make in comparison to how heavenly it tastes. I find fried cheese so satisfying as a snack or light meal.

MAKES 4 SERVINGS

———

3 tablespoons extra-virgin olive oil
4 ounces Caciocavallo cheese, cut into 4 slices
4 small, ripe plum tomatoes, seeded and chopped
Dried oregano to taste
Salt and freshly ground black pepper to taste

———

1. Heat the olive oil in a small cast-iron or other skillet over high heat. Add the slices of cheese, tomatoes, and a sprinkling of oregano, salt, and pepper.

2. Cook without turning until the cheese melts, about 2 minutes, then scrape onto a plate and serve.

Crocchetta

Croque monsieur, Italian style. This is a great quick sandwich where the strong taste of sheep cheese mingles nicely with the prosciutto.

MAKES 4 SMALL SERVINGS

————

8 slices round Italian- or French-style country bread
24 slices (about $^1/_2$ pound) prosciutto or coppa
8 slices (about 2 ounces) Fiore di Sardegna or any mild sheep's cheese
2 to 3 large eggs, beaten
$^1/_4$ cup ($^1/_2$ stick) unsalted butter

————

1. Divide the bread, prosciutto, and cheese into 4 equal portions and make a sandwich from each of them. Dip each sandwich into the eggs, coating both sides.

2. Melt the butter in a large skillet over a medium-high heat. Place the sandwiches in the pan. Flip them over when the bottoms have browned, about 4 minutes, and brown the other side. Serve immediately.

FIORE DI SARDEGNA CHEESE

This cheese is a version of Pecorino (page 61) made from sheep's milk on the island of Sardinia. Many Sardinian families still make their own Fiore di Sardegna cheese, and the markets in towns like Cagliari offer an astonishing array of them. They are sold in small wheels weighing about 4 pounds, and when young they are eaten as a table cheese or used for cooking. The cheese is soaked in brine and then dry salted. A good gourmet cheese store or an Italian market should carry it.

⌒

Bone marrow is a rich-tasting substance, known as collagen, found inside bones. In supermarkets these marrow-filled bones are often sold as "soup bones." You can use marrow as a cooking fat or like butter on bread, although its richness will keep you from eating too much. Have the bones at room temperature and scoop the marrow out using a small paring or dinner knife to cut into the marrow next to the bone. Use a demitasse or baby spoon to get whatever you can't get out with the knife. You may need to ask the butcher to split the bone for you if he hasn't already.

⌒

Veal Marrow Crostini

Perfect when you can't think of what to serve as an appetizer, accompaniment, or when you're plain too tired to cook. This is an old recipe that I learned from one of Ada Boni's cookbooks.

MAKES 20 CROSTINI; 10 SERVINGS

———

20 slices French bread
1¼ cups veal bone marrow (about 5 pounds bones), at
room temperature
Salt to taste

———

1. Preheat the oven to 400°F.

2. Arrange the slices of bread on a baking tray and spread the marrow over them with a knife or spoon. Bake until the marrow has melted, 6 to 7 minutes. Remove from the oven and serve with salt if desired.

Pancetta and Provolone Crostini

I thought these up one day when I realized dinner was going to be an hour later than I had expected and I knew the family would get hungry. I used a microwave and a toaster, although you can broil them, too.

MAKES 12 CROSTINI; 6 SERVINGS

———

12 slices French or Italian bread, lightly toasted
Twelve ¼-inch-thick slices mild Caciocavallo or provolone cheese, cut into 2-inch squares
12 very thin slices pancetta

———

1. Arrange the toasted bread on a platter. Arrange the slices of cheese on a baking sheet or microwave-safe tray and cover each with a slice of pancetta.

2. Microwave until the cheese is melted or place under a preheated broiler until the cheese is bubbling, 2 to 3 minutes.

3. Remove with a spatula and place on top of a bread slice and serve.

PROVOLONE

Provolone is a spun-curd type of cheese similar to Caciocavallo (page 10). It is formed into long pear or sausage shapes and strung together. The cheese is pale yellow on the outside and almost white on the inside. It is sold in mild and sharp varieties, the mild one used more often for cooking.

~

Fontina is a classic Italian cheese and the best comes from the Val d'Aosta region. Unfortunately, most of the imported Italian Fontina sold in this country is Valbella, which is of secondary quality but fine to use in any recipe. I can't recommend non-Italian Fontina.

Fontina is made from cow's milk into wheels weighing about twenty pounds that are dry salted. The rind of Fontina Val d'Aosta is thin and the cheese within soft and straw-colored with a few holes. The flavor is quite mellow and wonderful for eating as well as cooking because it melts well.

~

Fontina Crostini

Here is the quintessential snack. I first had this when my uncle Nathan Dellagatta, whose family is from Bari, made it for me more than twenty years ago. It's a classic. I usually make this in a toaster oven, as does Uncle Nat.

MAKES 1 SERVING

———

2 thin slices Fontina cheese
2 slices fresh or stale French or Italian bread

———

1. Preheat the oven to 350°F.

2. Put a slice of cheese on each slice of bread and set on a baking sheet. Place the bread in the oven until the cheese begins to bubble, about 10 minutes, and serve.

Tomato, Asparagus, and Hearts of Palm Panino

When I travel in Italy I love to buy a couple of panini—little sandwiches sold at cafes—for a mid-morning bite to eat. This particular panino might seem strange, but the tastes are naturally complementary and really very good with lots of mayonnaise.

MAKES 4 SERVINGS

———

8 small, soft rolls
16 stalks canned palm hearts, sliced lengthwise
3 ripe plum tomatoes, thinly sliced
16 stalks canned asparagus
Mayonnaise, preferably homemade, to taste

———

1. Slice the bread open. Divide the hearts of palm, tomatoes, and asparagus into 8 portions.

2. Coat each side of the bread with mayonnaise and layer the ingredients over the bottoms of the rolls. Put the tops on and press down gently.

Fagioli con Gamberetti

Beans and shrimp. Sounds so simple, but you will marvel at the summertime perfectness of this preparation. Serve it at room temperature with Grilled Wolffish (page 224).

MAKES 4 SERVINGS

---

4 to 6 ounces small shrimp

1 cup dried navy beans, soaked overnight in water to cover and drained

1/4 cup chopped red onion

2 ripe plum tomatoes, peeled, seeded, and chopped

1 large garlic clove, finely chopped

1/2 cup black Niçoise olives

1/4 cup extra-virgin olive oil

1 tablespoon finely chopped fresh basil leaves

Salt and freshly ground black pepper to taste

10 to 12 small fresh lemon basil leaves

---

1. Bring a 2- to 4-quart saucepan of lightly salted water to a boil. Place the shrimp in their shells into the boiling water and cook until orange, about 2½ minutes. Drain, let cool, then remove the shells and chop the shrimp. Set aside.

2. In the same pot, place the beans and water to cover. Bring to a boil, reduce the heat to medium, and simmer until tender, 45 minutes to 1 hour, then drain and cool.

3. Toss together the beans, shrimp, onion, tomatoes, garlic, olives, oil, and basil and season with salt and pepper. Let everything come to room temperatfure, garnish with the lemon basil leaves, and serve.

Pancetta and Tomato

Simple flavors can be astonishing, as this delicious combination illustrates. Microwaving is the fastest and most convenient way to prepare the pancetta, an Italian cured bacon.

MAKES 4 SERVINGS

———

8 slices (about ¹/₄ pound) pancetta
8 small soft rolls
3 ripe plum tomatoes, sliced
Extra-virgin olive oil for drizzling
Freshly ground black pepper to taste

———

1. Put the slices of pancetta between paper towels and microwave on medium power until crisp.

2. Slice open the rolls, lay the tomato slices on one side, and cover with the pancetta. Drizzle the olive oil on the other halves of the rolls and sprinkle some pepper on top of the tomatoes. Cover, press down gently, and serve.

CHAPTER TWO

Salads and Soups

ITALIAN FAMILIES USUALLY EAT their salad after dinner—it's a light and refreshing way to end a meal. When you have the salad before the main course, it's an appetizer, I think. Anyway, here are some easy salads for everyday cooking and one pasta salad for that potluck meal you've gotten yourself invited to.

A hearty soup is a truly satisfying home meal. I am much more of a soup eater in the winter. I love a hearty lentil minestrone soup when it's cold outside, but this chapter includes a perfect hot weather soup, too—Cold Milk and Lettuce Soup (page 34).

We now know that broccoli is one of the healthiest foods you can eat. But many people don't know how to cook broccoli. In fact, I believe the reason many people claim not to like broccoli is because Depression- and World War II–generation mothers regularly overcooked broccoli, which has the unfortunate result of releasing stinky compounds such as ammonia and hydrogen sulfide. Luckily, the Italians are masters of broccoli cookery (even the word *broccoli* is Italian) and there are some great recipes for broccoli (see the index).

Broccoli is best when picked young. The stalks should be rigid and solid, the florets tight and dark green. The floret branch should snap off when bent (this is, in fact, what the Italian word *broccoli* refers to, the small branches of the florets). Smell the

Broccoli and White Onion Salad

White rather than yellow onions are critical in this salad, not only for taste but also for color contrast. This salad also makes a very nice antipasto or *contorno*, accompaniment, to grilled or roast meat.

MAKES 6 TO 8 SERVINGS

―――――

3 pounds broccoli
1 medium-size white onion, chopped
Grated zest of 1 orange
1 tablespoon sugar
2 tablespoons white wine vinegar
¼ to ½ cup extra-virgin olive oil
1 teaspoon dried oregano
2 salted anchovy fillets, rinsed, patted dry, and finely chopped
1 garlic clove, finely chopped
Salt and freshly ground black pepper to taste
Orange wedges (optional) for garnish

―――――

1. Bring a pot of lightly salted water to a boil and plunge the broccoli in to blanch for 2 minutes. Drain and cool quickly in cold water. Return the broccoli to a steamer or strainer and steam in a covered pot over boiling water until tender but still maintaining a very slight crunch, about 8 minutes. Let the broccoli drain and cool in the strainer.

2. Break the broccoli into florets, saving the thick stems for another use, and toss with the onion and orange zest in a large mixing bowl.

3. In a small bowl, dissolve the sugar in the vinegar. Add the olive oil, oregano, anchovies, and garlic and whisk together well. Pour over the broccoli, season with salt and pepper, and toss again.

4. Transfer to a large serving platter and decorate with orange wedges, if desired. Serve at room temperature.

broccoli: there should be no odor but that of freshness. When broccoli is mature, it tastes woody and has an unpleasant smell when cooked.

Fresh broccoli should be stored in the refrigerator crisper drawer, unwashed until used. Cook broccoli the day you buy it or the day after. Cooked broccoli can be refrigerated for two days.

Wash broccoli before cooking, and cook according to the recipe, never longer. The stems are good to eat, either raw or cooked, and I often peel and julienne them for serving with a dip or plain with extra-virgin olive oil and a little salt. If boiling broccoli, it can be cooked whole or cut up, but remember that the florets will cook through before the stems. Blanching broccoli in boiling water for a couple of minutes will preserve its green color.

Green and Yellow Salad

The colors are startling in this zippy salad for a summer day. It's great with something off the grill and the leftovers are used in Baked Penne with Tomato and Anchovy Sauce (page 130).

MAKES 2 TO 4 SERVINGS

———

1 pound broccoli, broken into small florets
1 yellow bell pepper, seeded and chopped
Extra-virgin olive oil to taste
Coarse salt to taste
Freshly ground black pepper to taste

———

1. Steam the broccoli in a covered pot over boiling water until tender but still maintaining a slight crunch.

2. Drain well, toss with the yellow pepper and olive oil, and season with salt and pepper.

Simple Dandelion Salad

I love a simple salad after dinner, especially when I've had steak. Although many of our Italian grandfathers knew the delight of dandelions, for many Americans they are a new taste, slightly bitter, but light and fresh with a drizzle of fruity olive oil. If you don't have access to dandelions in your supermarket, you can harvest them from your backyard. They are best picked when the leaves are big but before any flower stem has appeared. Pick them, root and all, then wash, trim, and enjoy. The supermarket dandelions are cultivated, so their leaves will be longer. Remember that if you or the previous owner of your home has ever used pesticides on the lawn, you cannot use the dandelions.

MAKES 4 SERVINGS

―――――

1 bunch dandelions (about 1½ pounds), thoroughly washed, dried, and leaves ripped
Extra-virgin olive oil to taste
Balsamic vinegar (optional) to taste
Freshly grated Parmesan cheese (optional) to taste
Salt and freshly ground black pepper to taste

―――――

1. In a large bowl, toss the dandelions with the other ingredients.

2. Divide among 4 salad plates, top with some more olive oil, vinegar, and cheese, then season with salt and pepper and serve.

Sun Salad

Assemble this beautiful salad as you would a work of art. It's stunning to look at and eat. Choose vine-ripened juicy tomatoes and the best imported olives, not too bitter, not too salty.

MAKES 2 SERVINGS

———

2 large eggs, hard-boiled and shelled
2 ripe, but firm plum tomatoes (the same size as the eggs)
8 large imported black olives, pitted and sliced
1 tablespoon chopped fresh parsley leaves
Freshly squeezed lemon juice to taste
Salt and freshly ground black pepper to taste
Extra-virgin olive oil to taste

———

1. Slice the eggs and tomatoes into 7 slices each. Arrange the egg and tomato slices in concentric, overlapping rings on a small serving platter, so that a bit of yolk shows.

2. Sprinkle the olives and parsley around randomly. Squirt with some lemon juice, season with salt and pepper, drizzle with olive oil, and serve.

Tomato, Artichoke, and Montasio Salad with Green Sauce

Montasio cheese is a mild whole cow's milk cheese from the Friuli region of northeastern Italy, made during the summer pasturage in the Alps. The cheese is smooth without many holes. It is salted in a weak brine and eaten as a table cheese when young. Montasio is sold in Italian markets or specialty cheese shops, but can be replaced with Fontina. If you intend on having another course, try Grilled Tuna with Salsa Verde (page 220), which uses the same sauce.

MAKES 4 SERVINGS

8 very ripe plum tomatoes (about 1 pound), cut into eighths
4 imported marinated artichoke hearts, cut into eighths
¼ pound Montasio cheese, diced
Salt and freshly ground black pepper to taste

FOR THE GREEN SAUCE
2 tablespoons very finely chopped fresh parsley leaves
1 small garlic clove, very finely chopped
3 tablespoons extra-virgin olive oil

1. Toss the tomatoes, artichokes, and cheese together. Season with salt and pepper and toss again.

2. Mix the sauce ingredients and sprinkle over the salad. Set aside to serve at room temperature.

Tomato, Fava, Olive, and Mozzarella Salad

Fava bean pods are large and easily peeled, so don't let the peeling put you off. The flavor of fresh favas graced with a fruity olive oil and seasoned with basil leaves and garlic is worth the effort.

MAKES 2 TO 4 SERVINGS

———

1¹/₂ cups shelled fresh fava beans (about 2 pounds fava bean pods)
¹/₄ cup extra-virgin olive oil
1 garlic clove, very finely chopped
8 ripe plum tomatoes (about 1 pound), quartered
¹/₄ pound fresh mozzarella cheese, diced
1 cup imported black Gaeta or other black olives
1 tablespoon very finely chopped fresh basil leaves
Salt and freshly ground black pepper to taste

———

1. Bring a pot of lightly salted water to a boil and boil the fava beans until almost tender, about 5 minutes. Stir the olive oil and garlic together in a small bowl.

2. While the beans are cooking, place the tomatoes, cheese, and olives in the salad bowl or platter, and pour the olive oil and garlic over them.

3. Remove the fava beans from the now purple water and rinse with cold water. Peel the beans by pinching a small hole out of the opposite end from the side with the now-black seam and squeeze. The bean will pop out. Put them directly into the salad as you go. Toss the salad well, sprinkle with the basil, salt, and pepper, and serve.

Tomato and Gorgonzola Salad

Delicate and creamy, Gorgonzola is an Italian blue-type mold cheese made from cow's milk. It should be soft to the touch and the blue veins of mold quite obvious. Taste before buying; it should not be bitter, but rich with a sharp flavor. Ripe tomatoes and Gorgonzola make a nice accompaniment to grilled foods or any other simple food.

MAKES 2 TO 4 SERVINGS

———

1 large, very ripe tomato (about $^3/_4$ pound)
$^1/_4$ cup Gorgonzola cheese, at room temperature
1 teaspoon finely chopped fresh basil leaves
Salt and freshly ground black pepper to taste
Extra-virgin olive oil

———

1. Cut the tomato into 4 thick slices and arrange on a serving platter.

2. Smear about 1 tablespoon of the Gorgonzola on each slice and sprinkle with the basil, salt, and pepper. Drizzle with olive oil and serve at room temperature.

Arugula is a salad green, also called rocket, that belongs to the same family as broccoli. It is popular among Italians and increasingly found everywhere in this country. It is a sharp-tasting green and an excellent way to add flavor to various preparations. Its flat leaves and long stems look like those of dandelions.

Boston Lettuce and Arugula Salad with Walnuts

This is a nice salad to have with another dish, perhaps a simple pasta or chicken preparation. The walnuts and cheese make the salad complete.

MAKES 4 SERVINGS

———

1 head Boston lettuce, washed, dried, and leaves ripped
20 large arugula leaves, washed, dried, and leaves ripped
6 cherry tomatoes
8 bocconcini (cherry-sized mozzarella balls), or $^1/_3$ pound fresh mozzarella, cubed
$^1/_3$ cup chopped walnuts
8 imported black olives

FOR THE VINAIGRETTE
$^1/_4$ cup extra-virgin olive oil
1 tablespoon red wine vinegar
1 tablespoon finely chopped fresh basil leaves
1 garlic clove, finely chopped

———

1. Arrange the lettuce and arugula leaves on a platter. Sprinkle the cherry tomatoes, bocconcini, walnuts, and olives over them.

2. Whisk the vinaigrette ingredients together and pour over the salad.

Carrot and Radicchio Salad

A refreshing, very simple salad of julienned carrots and slightly bitter red radicchio that you can put together while the meat cooks—for instance, Sear-Crusted Thyme and White Pepper Steak (page 184).

MAKES 2 SERVINGS

————

¹/₂ pound carrots, peeled and julienned
1 head radicchio, trimmed of tough stems and sliced into strips
Salt and freshly ground black pepper to taste
Extra-virgin olive oil to taste

————

1. Arrange the carrots and radicchio attractively on a serving platter.

2. Season with salt and pepper, drizzle with olive oil, and serve.

NOTE: The carrot can be julienned with the proper food processor blade or bought from the salad bar of many supermarkets.

Soffritto is an Italian cooking term I use often in this book, even if many Italian Americans do not. It's a dandy term that, at its most basic, describes a sauté of finely chopped onions in olive oil. Although most Italian-English dictionaries translate soffritto as "sauté," it really means to fry very gently, to underfry (*sotto friggere*). A soffritto is often the beginning of a sauce or more involved preparation. A more complex soffritto would also include finely chopped garlic, celery, or herbs, usually parsley. As the onions begin to turn translucent, tomatoes, or whatever else the dish requires, such as meat or vegetables, are added. Soffritto, besides being a foundation to a sauce, is also a flavorful aromatic.

∽

A Really Spectacular Potluck Pasta and Vegetable Salad

Potluck dishes have a bad reputation because cooks tend to slap anything together without thought, rather than preparing something to showcase their talents. Well, this pasta salad tastes great and takes no time at all. Garden-fresh vegetables are cooked quickly and tossed with a savory and pungent soffritto, a complementary flavor to the penne or macaroni. The beets provide beautiful red streaks throughout, as well as a nice taste. Save the beet leaves to make Orecchiette with Beet Leaves, Tuna, and Olives (page 135).

To keep the preparation from becoming greasy, make sure your frying oil has reached the proper temperature before cooking the vegetables.

MAKES 8 SERVINGS

———

6 cups olive oil for frying
3 small beets, peeled and cut into french fry shapes
Salt
3/4 pound broccoli (about 1 1/2 stalks), broken into florets and the stems peeled and julienned
2 celery stalks, thinly sliced diagonally
1 medium-size yellow summer squash, peeled, seeded, and thinly sliced
1 pound penne or macaroni
1 orange bell pepper, charred over a burner or grill or under a broiler, seeded, and partially peeled
14 imported green olives, pitted and chopped
6 fresh basil leaves, finely chopped
1 garlic clove, finely chopped

2 tablespoons pine nuts
2 salted anchovy fillets, rinsed and patted dry
½ cup extra-virgin olive oil
Freshly ground black pepper to taste

―――――

1. Preheat the frying oil in a deep fryer to 375°F or in an 8-inch saucepan over medium-high heat until almost smoking, about 10 minutes.

2. Deep-fry the beets without crowding them in the fryer or pan (you may have to do this in several batches) until crispy looking, 7 to 8 minutes. Remove from the oil with a slotted spoon, drain a bit, and set aside in a large paper towel-lined mixing bowl to further drain, salting lightly immediately. Deep-fry the broccoli, without crowding, until the edges turn brown, about 3 minutes. Remove with a slotted spoon, drain, and set aside in the paper towel-lined bowl, salting lightly immediately. Deep-fry the celery for 1 minute, remove, drain, and add to the bowl. Deep-fry the squash until the edges turn brown, about 2 minutes, remove, drain, and set aside in the bowl.

3. Meanwhile, bring a large pot of abundantly salted water to a rolling boil, add the pasta, cook until al dente, and drain.

4. Cut the bell pepper into strips, then cut each strip into 4 pieces. Remove the paper toweling from the bowl and add the pasta and pepper.

5. In a small skillet, heat the olives, basil, garlic, pine nuts, anchovies, and ½ cup olive oil over medium-high heat for 1 to 2 minutes after it first starts to sizzle. Pour the sauce over the pasta mixture and toss well. Season with salt and pepper and leave until it reaches room temperature before serving. Let the frying oil cool, then strain and save.

BEETS

~

When shopping for fresh beets, look for equal-sized bunches with fresh, crisp-looking green, not yellowish, leaves. Do not choose very big beet roots, as they will have a woody taste. The best are small beets about two inches in diameter at the most, although these are difficult to find since the farmer must pull them early. The surfaces should be free of blemishes and the flesh hard without soft spots. Store beets in the refrigerator crisper drawer for up to two weeks, although the leaves must be eaten within two days.

When cooking beets, cook them whole, trimmed of their leaves but not of their stems, unless the recipe instructs you otherwise. When working with fresh beets, make sure clothing is protected because the juice will stain.

~

Potato, Saffron, and Watercress Soup

This creamy vegetable soup, gaily laced with saffron, is mellow and perfect as a cold-weather lunch dish. Leftovers freeze well.

MAKES 4 SERVINGS

6 cups cold water
3 tablespoons extra-virgin olive oil
1 medium-size boiling potato, peeled and finely chopped
2 ripe plum tomatoes, peeled, seeded, and finely chopped
1 small Italian long pepper (peperoncini), seeded and finely chopped
1 small onion, finely chopped
Bouquet garni consisting of a bunch of watercress and 8 fresh sage leaves, tied together in cheesecloth
Salt and freshly ground black pepper to taste
1/2 pound Fontina cheese, cut into tiny dice
Pinch of saffron threads, crumbled
Heavy cream to taste

1. Pour the cold water and olive oil into a large saucepan and turn the heat to high. Add the potato, tomatoes, pepper, and onion; stir, and add the bouquet garni. Season with salt and pepper, then add the cheese and saffron. Cook until the potatoes are tender but not falling apart, 12 to 14 minutes, stirring almost constantly, then add cream to your taste and correct the salt and pepper, if necessary. Discard the bouquet garni and serve the soup in individual bowls.

Swiss Chard Stalk Soup

Frugal Italian home cooks don't throw away the white stalks of Swiss chard but use them in a variety of preparations. One of the best is this farmhouse-style soup. Save the green leaves to make Swiss Chard with Mascarpone-Gorgonzola Gratinate (page 238).

MAKES 4 SERVINGS

2 tablespoons extra-virgin olive oil
3 garlic cloves, finely chopped
½ pound Swiss chard stalks, chopped
4 cups chicken broth
Salt and freshly ground black pepper to taste
¼ cup freshly grated Parmesan cheese

1. Heat the olive oil in a saucepan over high heat. Add the garlic and Swiss chard stalks and cook until the chard softens just a bit, about 2 minutes, stirring frequently so the garlic doesn't burn.

2. Pour in the chicken broth and season with salt and pepper. Bring to a boil, reduce the heat to medium, and boil gently until the stalks are tender. Ladle into 4 bowls and add a tablespoon of Parmesan cheese to each.

VARIATION: Add a beaten egg during the last minute of cooking and serve with a toasted slice of olive oil-brushed Italian bread.

Cold Milk and Lettuce Soup

This Italianate twist on the classic French vichyssoise is an especially pleasant lunch soup for a very hot summer day. Often I don't feel like eating much when it is too hot, yet I still get hungry for something effortless and savory. This cold milk soup was ideal on a day when the temperature hit 98°F.

MAKES 2 SERVINGS

---

1 tablespoon unsalted butter
1 tablespoon extra-virgin olive oil
1 garlic clove, crushed
1 head Boston lettuce, washed, dried, and leaves chopped
Salt and freshly ground black pepper to taste
1 tablespoon dry white wine
2 cups whole or 2% milk

---

1. In a large skillet, heat the butter with the olive oil along with the garlic over medium heat. When the bubbles of the butter subside, add the lettuce, season with salt and pepper, and cook, stirring, until the lettuce wilts, about 1 minute. Add the wine and cook another minute.

2. Take the skillet off the heat and divide the lettuce between 2 bowls. Pour a cup of the milk in each, stir, and serve.

Chicken Heart Soup

This is a hearty (!) soup that cooks quickly because the hearts are so small. Supermarkets will occasionally sell hearts separately from the gizzards, which is ideal for this preparation, and just about the only way you can make it, given how many hearts you'll need. Otherwise you'll simply have to save and freeze the hearts over a period of time to get enough to make this delicious soup.

MAKES 4 SERVINGS

———

6 cups chicken broth, preferably homemade
4 dried red chili peppers (optional)
1½ pounds chicken hearts
1 cup shredded carrots
½ cup chopped fresh basil leaves
⅔ cup medium-grain rice (also known as Spanish rice)
⅔ cup tubettini
Pinch of ground coriander
Salt and freshly ground black pepper to taste
Freshly grated Pecorino cheese to taste

———

1. Bring the chicken broth to a boil in a large saucepan with the chili peppers. Add the chicken hearts, carrots, and basil and boil for 15 minutes.

2. Add the rice and cook for 7 minutes. Add the tubettini and coriander, season with salt and pepper, and boil until the rice is tender, about 8 more minutes. Serve with a sprinkling of cheese.

Cod and Acini di Pepe Soup

All kinds of special pastas used only for soups are sold in Italian markets. Supermarkets carry some, too, but usually not as wide of a variety. Acini di pepe, literally "peppercorns," is a dry soup pasta the size of peppercorns, hence the name, and perfect for this soup.

In New England, pieces of cod, haddock, or pollack are sold as chowder fish, and this is what you want when you make this soup, using whatever local fish is available, freshest, and usually cheapest.

MAKES 4 TO 6 SERVINGS

———

3 tablespoons extra-virgin olive oil
¹⁄₂ fennel bulb, thoroughly washed and finely chopped
1 garlic clove, finely chopped
¹⁄₂ small onion, finely chopped
¹⁄₄ cup finely chopped fresh parsley leaves
1 small, ripe plum tomato, peeled, seeded, and finely chopped
4 cups cold water
10 ounces cod or any inexpensive local fish, cut into pieces
¹⁄₄ cup dry soup pasta (such as acini di pepe or stelline)
1 dried red chili pepper
4 salted anchovy fillets, rinsed and patted dry
1 teaspoon salt
Freshly ground black pepper to taste

———

1. In a large saucepan, heat the olive oil over high heat and cook the fennel, onion, and garlic together until soft, about 2 minutes, stirring constantly so the garlic doesn't burn. Add the parsley and

cook for 1 minute, stirring. Add the tomato and cook another minute.

2. Pour in the water, bring to a boil, then add the fish, pasta, chili pepper, salt, and pepper and reduce the heat to medium. Cook until the pasta is al dente and the fish begins to flake, about 10 minutes. Taste, correct the seasoning, and serve.

Easy Lentil Minestrone

Although canned or concentrated chicken bouillon is fine for this recipe, be careful when seasoning because commercial broths are often high in sodium.

The pasta used in this recipe is called *tubettini,* or little tubes, the smallest in the family of tubular macaroni. They are usually sold among other "soup" pastas. Red lentils are usually found in Middle Eastern markets or whole food stores. Use brown lentils in their place.

MAKES 3 TO 4 SERVINGS

———

8 cups chicken broth, preferably homemade
1/2 cup dried red lentils
1/4 pound tubettini (about 1/2 cup)
Freshly grated Parmesan cheese to taste

———

1. Bring the chicken broth to a boil.

2. Add the lentils and continue to boil until they are soft, about 15 minutes, then add the tubettini. Boil until the tubettini are al dente, then sprinkle in the cheese. Serve immediately.

CHAPTER THREE

Frittate

"SO YOU MADE A FRITTATA?" I asked. "Well, I made an omelet," answered my friend, "because I flipped it over." Well, that's the difference between a frittata and an omelet. A frittata is actually very close to what the Spanish call a *tortilla*—an omelet that is slid under a broiler until it sets and served flat as an antipasto (or tapas in Spain) or, as among Italian families, a light lunch, a midnight snack, or an accompaniment to a soup or even cold in a sandwich. But the biggest difference between an omelet and a frittata is that a frittata is not usually a breakfast item, as is the omelet. The ones here are all family favorites and they're pretty easy to do. Before you start, heat the broiler and when it comes time to stick the skillet in there, you may need to keep the oven door open a bit because the handle won't fit. Don't worry about that—just go ahead and do it (it stays in there less than 2 minutes) and you'll have a fine frittata. And if you flip it over on itself, you'll have an omelet!

Just as with a perfect omelet, a frittata is best when made small, usually one or two servings made from three or four eggs. This is why using a nonstick skillet is best—you can quickly make servings in rapid sequence without struggling with a pan to clean.

Scallion and Mint Frittata

Fragrant scallions flavor this fluffy frittata seasoned with fresh mint. It can even be served at room temperature.

MAKES 1 SERVING

———

2 tablespoons extra-virgin olive oil
3 scallions, chopped
1 tablespoon chopped fresh mint leaves
2 large eggs, beaten until frothy
Salt and freshly ground black pepper to taste

———

1. Preheat the broiler.

2. Heat the olive oil in a nonstick omelet pan over medium-high heat. Cook the scallions and mint, stirring, for 1 minute, then pour in the beaten eggs and season with salt and pepper. Once the bottom sets, 30 seconds to 1 minute, remove the pan from the burner and place under the broiler until the top is almost set, another 30 seconds to 1 minute.

3. Remove, slide the frittata onto a plate, folding it over if desired, and serve.

Mushroom Frittata

The rich taste of this frittata comes from the dark, meaty, earthy-tasting portobello mushroom.

MAKES 1 SERVING

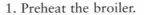

2 tablespoons extra-virgin olive oil
1 portobello mushroom cap, any size, thinly sliced
3 large eggs, beaten until frothy
Salt to taste
2 tablespoons freshly grated Parmesan cheese
Finely chopped fresh parsley leaves (optional) for a garnish

1. Preheat the broiler.

2. Heat the olive oil in a nonstick omelet pan over medium-high heat and cook the mushroom until moist and dark looking, about 8 minutes, stirring frequently. Pour in the eggs, add salt, and sprinkle the cheese on top. Once the bottom sets, 30 seconds to 1 minute, remove from the burner and place under the broiler until the top sets, another 30 seconds to 1 minute.

3. Remove, slide the frittata onto a plate, folding it over if desired, and serve with a sprinkle of parsley.

Fluffy Parsley Frittata

By separating the eggs, you get a very fluffy frittata that is ideal for pairing with fresh herbs.

MAKES 1 SERVING

———

3 large eggs, separated
Salt and freshly ground black pepper to taste
2 tablespoons unsalted butter
1/4 cup chopped fresh parsley leaves, or more to taste

———

1. Preheat the broiler.

2. Beat the egg whites until very frothy but not peaked. In another bowl, beat the egg yolks with the salt and pepper. Fold the egg whites into the yolks and beat until the mixture is a light yellow froth.

3. In a nonstick omelet pan, melt the butter over medium-high heat and pour the eggs into the pan. Once the bottom has set, 30 seconds to 1 minute, remove from the burner, sprinkle with the parsley, and place under the broiler until the top sets, another 30 seconds to 1 minute.

4. Remove, slide the frittata onto a plate, folding it over if desired, and serve.

Although everyone, including myself, calls oregano the quintessential Italian herb, perhaps that appellation best belongs to parsley. Parsley is versatile, in everything from soups to sauces to garnish (there is hardly a dish in Italy that doesn't leave the restaurant kitchen with a sprinkle of finely chopped parsley). Parsley is also an easy herb for the garden. There are two varieties usually available in the market: curly leaf and flat leaf (also called Italian parsley). You guessed it; use the flat-leaf variety in my recipes. But there is another reason besides its name—it's less bitter than the curly leaf.

Only fresh parsley will do in all these recipes because dried parsley is tasteless and without aroma. Do not wash parsley until needed and dry it before chopping.

Asiago is a semi-hard, dry salted or brined cow's milk cheese. It is usually eaten when four to six months old and is used for cooking, especially grated. Asiago is made in wheels a little more than a foot in diameter and about four inches thick. The taste is delicate because of its young age but it grows stronger as it gets older. The cheese is straw colored, punctuated evenly with small holes.

Asiago is usually found in Italian markets, quality cheese stores, and in some supermarkets.

❧

Pine Nut, Red Bell Pepper, and Asiago Cheese Frittata

This flavorful frittata is best made with roasted red bell peppers preserved in olive oil. The Asiago, if you can't find it, can be replaced with a Spanish Manchego cheese or Italian provolone. Serve with some crusty bread to soak up the olive oil and capture the pine nuts.

MAKES 1 SERVING

———

2 tablespoons extra-virgin olive oil
4 teaspoons pine nuts
1 freshly roasted or jarred red bell pepper, chopped
3 large eggs
3 tablespoons freshly grated Asiago cheese
Salt and freshly ground black pepper to taste
Finely chopped fresh parsley leaves (optional)

———

1. Preheat the broiler.

2. In a nonstick omelet pan, heat the olive oil over medium heat and sauté the pine nuts until light brown, about 3 minutes, stirring or shaking the pan. Add the roasted pepper and heat for 30 seconds.

3. In a small bowl, beat the eggs until frothy with the cheese, salt, and pepper and pour into the pan. Cook until the bottom sets, 30 seconds to 1 minute. Remove the pan from the burner and place under the broiler until the top sets, another 30 seconds to 1 minute.

4. Remove, slide the frittata onto a plate, folding it over if desired, sprinkle with parsley, if desired, and serve.

Ham, Cheese, and Tomato Frittata

Cooking the ham in pancetta fat and olive oil sure does provide a rustic flavor, and it's a taste I love, even if I don't eat it often.

MAKES 1 SERVING

————

2 tablespoons extra-virgin olive oil
1 tablespoon finely chopped pancetta or pork fatback
2 ounces cooked ham, finely chopped
1 ripe plum tomato, finely chopped
3 large eggs, beaten until frothy
Salt and freshly ground black pepper to taste
2 to 3 ounces Taleggio, Fontina, or Brie cheese, thinly sliced
1 tablespoon finely chopped fresh parsley leaves

————

1. Preheat the broiler.

2. In a nonstick omelet pan, heat the olive oil over a medium-high heat and cook the pancetta, ham, and tomato together until the pancetta is soft and the tomato has emitted some liquid, about 4 minutes, stirring occasionally. Pour in the eggs and season with salt and pepper. Arrange the cheese on top, sprinkle with the parsley, and once the bottom is set, 30 seconds to 1 minute, remove from the burner and place under the broiler until the top has set, another 30 to 60 seconds.

3. Remove, slide the frittata onto a plate, folding it over if desired, and serve.

Goat Cheese, Almond, and Pecorino Frittata

You may have trouble finding an Italian variety of fresh goat cheese. If that's the case, try any fresh or young goat cheese sold by your supermarket or cheese store.

This recipe always reminds me of the sylvan food of shepherd families found in the high pastureland of Alpine Italy.

MAKES 2 SERVINGS

———

3 tablespoons extra-virgin olive oil
24 blanched whole almonds
8 cherry tomatoes, quartered
4 large eggs, beaten until frothy
$1/4$ cup crumbled fresh goat cheese
$1/4$ cup freshly grated Pecorino cheese
1 tablespoon finely chopped fresh parsley leaves

———

1. Preheat the broiler.

2. Heat the olive oil in a nonstick omelet pan over medium heat and sauté the almonds until light brown, about 3 minutes, stirring or shaking the pan. Add the tomatoes and cook until soft but still maintaining their shape, another 6 minutes, stirring. Pour in the eggs, season with salt and pepper, and sprinkle the goat cheese over the top. Sprinkle with the Pecorino and once the bottom has set, 30 seconds to 1 minute, remove from the burner and place under the broiler until the top sets, another 30 seconds to 1 minute.

3. Remove, slide the frittata onto a plate, folding it over if desired, sprinkle with the parsley, and serve.

Sausage, Mozzarella, and Tomato Sauce Frittata

This is a fast-lunch frittata that utilizes any leftover tomato sauce from Spaghetti with Tomato Sauce (page 54). If you haven't any left-over homemade sauce, use canned crushed tomatoes but not canned tomato sauce.

MAKES 2 SERVINGS

———

4 large eggs
Salt to taste
1 mild Italian sausage link, casing removed and meat crumbled
1/4 cup dry white wine
1/4 cup tomato sauce or crushed tomatoes
1 ounce fresh mozzarella, sliced

———

1. Preheat the broiler.

2. Beat the eggs and salt together in a bowl until frothy.

3. In a nonstick omelet pan, cook the crumbled sausage meat over high heat until it loses all pinkness, about 2 minutes, stirring and breaking up the sausage. Pour in the wine and let it evaporate, about 1 minute. Pour in the eggs, immediately spread some tomato sauce around, and layer the mozzarella on top. Once the bottom sets, 30 seconds to 1 minute, remove from the burner and place under the broiler until the top sets, about 60 seconds.

4. Remove, slide the frittata onto a plate, folding it over if desired, and serve.

Pine Nut, Peas, and Anchovy Frittata

I like this frittata for lunch. It's not heavy, yet the taste is bold enough to satisfy.

MAKES 1 SERVING

———

1 tablespoon extra-virgin olive oil
1 tablespoon pine nuts
3 large eggs, beaten until frothy
Salt and freshly ground black pepper to taste
1/4 cup cooked fresh peas (do not use canned)
Freshly grated Parmesan cheese to taste
4 salted anchovy fillets, rinsed and patted dry

———

1. Preheat the broiler.

2. Heat the olive oil in a nonstick omelet pan over medium-high heat and add the pine nuts. As the pine nuts begin to lightly brown, pour in the eggs and season with salt and pepper. Sprinkle on the peas and cheese, and lay the anchovy fillets on top. Once the bottom sets, 30 seconds to 1 minute, remove the pan from the burner and place under the broiler until the top is set, another 30 seconds to 1 minute.

3. Remove, slide the frittata onto a plate, folding it over if desired, and serve.

Ricotta and Sardine Frittata

Every once in a while my fishmonger has fresh whole sardines. I buy a bunch, gut them, and hope to find some roe, which I separate and freeze in order to make this quick frittata at a later time. Of course, if sardine roe is not available you can either use canned sardines or—and this may seem a little bizarre—a tablespoon of tarama, or carp roe, which is used in making the Greek dip known as taramasalata.

MAKES 1 SERVING

———

3 tablespoons ricotta cheese, preferably fresh
3 large eggs, beaten until frothy
Salt to taste
1½ tablespoons unsalted butter
3 tablespoons sardine roe or pieces of canned sardine
1 small garlic clove, finely chopped
Freshly ground black pepper to taste

———

1. Preheat the broiler.

2. Beat the ricotta into the eggs and season with salt.

3. In a nonstick omelet pan, melt the butter over medium-high heat and cook the sardine roe or pieces and garlic for 2 minutes, stirring constantly. Pour in the egg mixture. Once the bottom sets, 30 seconds to 1 minute, remove the pan from the burner and place under the broiler until the top sets, another 30 to 60 seconds. Season with pepper.

4. Remove, slide the frittata onto a plate, folding it over if desired, and serve.

BUTTER

Very little butter is used in Italian cooking. The much healthier olive oil is the favorite cooking fat. But some recipes do call for butter, and I always use unsalted (sweet) butter. I don't care for margarine and other butter substitutes. Italians do not serve butter with bread, preferring to use bread to soak up delicious sauces or for dipping in extra virgin olive oil. Try it!

Pasta
with Vegetables

ITALIAN-AMERICAN FAMILIES used to call pasta macaroni. My friend Nancy Verde Barr wrote a beautiful book-length ode to this cooking, called *We Called It Macaroni*. Perhaps you call it noodles.

The widest, most exciting pastas are found in Italian markets. Northern Italians favor egg pastas while southern Italians tend toward dried pastas made only with hard wheat and water, called *pastasciutta* or *pasta secca*, both words literally meaning "dry pasta." An Italian family uses fresh pasta (*pasta fresca*) and dry pasta (*pasta secca*) for two different purposes. Fresh pasta is not better than dry pasta. Fresh pastas were never meant to be trendy, as they have become in America, but are used for particular sauces and particular tastes. After the pasta dough is mixed and rolled out, it can be cooked and eaten immediately—this is fresh pasta. If it is set aside to dry, a process expedited by machines in pasta factories, then it is dried pasta.

There is only one correct method of cooking pasta. For every pound of pasta, you need five to six quarts of water and a tablespoon of salt. The water must be boiling furiously as you put the pasta into the water in ¼-pound increments rather quickly. Swirl the water so the pasta doesn't stick together at first. There is no point in adding oil to the water to accomplish this because oil and water separate, as you know, and therefore the oil will rise to the top and accomplish nothing. After the pasta has been cooking for the time suggested on the package, taste a strand to see if it is al dente. As you've been told a million times, *al dente* means "to the teeth," meaning the pasta should have a pleasant little bite to it. Then it's done and you can drain. Do not rinse pasta after draining; this will only wash away nutrients and the slight starchiness that allows sauces to bind.

If you are tempted to cook pasta in less water than recommended because the water will come to a boil quicker, be warned that the pasta, which releases starch when cooking, will turn out stickier and starchier—an unpleasant and un-Italian result.

Spaghetti with Fennel

This recipe may look too simple to try, but if you use very, very fresh vegetables you will be amazed at how these everyday ingredients can impart so much flavor and taste. This dish can be made with canned tomatoes, but is much better with juicy, ripe, and fresh tomatoes.

MAKES 4 SERVINGS

———

1/4 cup extra-virgin olive oil
1 cup very finely chopped onion
2 garlic cloves, finely chopped
1 cup very finely chopped fennel bulb
6 to 8 very ripe plum tomatoes (about 3/4 pound), peeled
Salt and freshly ground black pepper to taste
3/4 pound spaghetti
Freshly grated Parmesan cheese to taste

———

1. Heat the olive oil in a large skillet or casserole over medium heat and cook the onion, garlic, and fennel until soft, about 6 minutes, stirring frequently. Add the tomatoes, season with salt and pepper, and cook until most of the water from the tomatoes has evaporated, about 10 minutes.

2. Meanwhile, bring a large pot of abundantly salted water to a rolling boil and add the pasta. Drain when al dente. Pour the pasta into the skillet and toss well with the cheese and sauce until well coated.

Imagine Italian cooking without the tomato. Before Columbus there was no tomato in Italy. In fact, it wasn't until the late nineteenth century that the tomato became commonplace in Italian cooking.

There are many kinds of tomatoes, but in Italian family cooking the most popular is the San Marzano plum tomato, used for pastas and sauces, as well as the small round and sweet Principe Borghese. In these recipes I assume you'll be using fresh, vine-ripened tomatoes. But if tomatoes are not in season, then canned tomatoes are very good and preferable to a tasteless hothouse tomato. Many Italian families still keep a separate room, perhaps a garden shed, a garage space, or a walk-in closet, where they store jars upon jars of tomatoes from their abundant gardens and bottles

Spaghetti with Tomato Sauce

I'm a bit embarrassed about the title of this recipe—but that's what it is. I made this for friends once and they all asked for the recipe. Upon receiving it, they were disappointed that something so delicious was so simple to make. But then I remembered why it tasted so good. The tomatoes came from my garden. I let my tomatoes ripen on the vine, or until they fall off when lightly tapped.

This preparation is great with Grilled Skewers of Swordfish and Orange (page 214).

MAKES 4 SERVINGS

⎯⎯⎯⎯

¼ cup extra-virgin olive oil
2 garlic cloves, 1 crushed and 1 finely chopped
1 medium-size onion, finely chopped
2 tablespoons finely chopped fresh parsley leaves
2 pounds very ripe plum tomatoes
Salt and freshly ground black pepper to taste
1 pound spaghetti
Cayenne pepper (optional)

⎯⎯⎯⎯

1. In a large skillet or casserole, heat the olive oil over medium-high heat and cook the crushed garlic until it begins to turn light brown, about 1 minute. Remove and discard the garlic. Add the chopped garlic, onion, and parsley and cook over medium-high heat until the onion is soft, about 5 minutes, stirring constantly so the garlic doesn't burn. Add the tomatoes and season with salt and pepper. Reduce the heat to low and cook until thickened, about 15 minutes.

2. Meanwhile, bring a large pot of abundantly salted water to a rolling boil and add the pasta. Drain when al dente and toss together with the sauce in the skillet. Sprinkle some cayenne over if desired and serve.

upon bottles of homemade tomato sauce or puree. You will notice in Italy that every family seems to have some little plot of land, no matter how small, where they grow tomatoes, at least. Even in urban areas terra-cotta potted tomatoes will sit on balconies, capturing the last rays of sunlight.

~

Parmesan (Parmigiano-Reggiano) cheese is an aged, hard grating cheese made from cow's milk that is used in cooking and freshly grated on pasta. Only cheese makers in the province of Parma have been granted the right to call their Parmesan "Parmigiano-Reggiano," and it is so stamped on the rinds of the huge wheels of cheese that can reach fifty pounds. Low in fat and possessing a flaky texture, Parmigiano-Reggiano must be aged for two years before it can be sold.

American cheese producers make Parmesan cheese, but the Italian product is far superior. When shopping for Parmesan cheese, always buy a large chunk and keep it wrapped in plastic in the refrigerator. Grate the Parmesan as needed for fullest flavor. Avoid buying grated Parmesan in a con-

Penne with Tomato and Celery Sauce

Those brilliant red vine-ripened plum tomatoes that I pluck from my garden almost beg to be turned into a sauce for macaroni. In this recipe the basic tomato is enriched with the flavor of an onion, celery, and garlic soffritto (page 30) and then a reduction sauce is made with a full-bodied red wine. It's a terrific, honest pasta dish with the celery and oregano only hinting at their presence.

MAKES 4 TO 6 SERVINGS

———

1/4 cup extra-virgin olive oil
1 medium-size onion, chopped
1 celery stalk, sliced
2 garlic cloves, finely chopped
2 large, very ripe tomatoes (about 1 pound), peeled, seeded, and chopped
1 teaspoon dried oregano
Salt and freshly ground black pepper to taste
1/2 cup dry red wine
1 pound penne
Freshly grated Parmesan cheese to taste

———

1. In a large skillet or casserole, heat the olive oil over medium heat and cook the onion, celery, and garlic, stirring, until soft, about 5 minutes. Add the tomatoes and oregano, season with salt and pepper, reduce the heat to medium-low, and cook, stirring a few times, for 5 minutes. Pour in the wine and cook, stirring occasionally, until it is reduced and the sauce is thick, about 15 minutes.

2. Meanwhile, bring a large pot of abundantly salted water to a rolling boil and add the pasta. Drain when al dente and toss with the sauce in the skillet. Serve with abundant Parmesan cheese.

Penne with Celery Heart and Peperoncini

Peperoncini is a mild green pepper also known as an Italian long pepper. In this preparation the peperoncini is part of a soffritto made with celery heart, zucchini, and garlic. This base of fresh vegetables becomes aromatic with garlic, mint, red pepper, and a little tomato added for color and taste. The chili pepper gives the dish a nice bite. I especially like to eat room-temperature leftovers the next day.

MAKES 4 SERVINGS

———

2 tablespoons extra-virgin olive oil
1/2 cup finely chopped celery heart (the base of the innermost stalks)
1 cup finely chopped zucchini
1/2 cup seeded and finely chopped peperoncini
2 tablespoons finely chopped fresh mint leaves
2 garlic cloves, finely chopped
1 dried red chili pepper, seeded and crumbled
1 cup chopped fresh tomatoes
Salt and freshly ground black pepper to taste
1/2 pound penne
Freshly grated Parmesan cheese to taste

———

1. Heat the olive oil in a large skillet or casserole over medium-high heat and cook the celery heart, zucchini, peperoncini, mint, garlic,

tainer; once the cheese is grated it loses its freshness and taste.

Italian home cooks save the rinds of the cheese and use them to flavor minestrone and stews.

and chili pepper until slightly soft, about 4 minutes, stirring occasionally. Reduce the heat to medium-low, add the tomatoes, season with salt and pepper, cover, and simmer until rich and aromatic, about 15 minutes, stirring occasionally.

2. Meanwhile, bring a large pot of abundantly salted water to a rolling boil and add the pasta. Drain when al dente and pour into the skillet with the sauce. Toss well and serve with cheese.

CHICK-PEAS

Chick-peas are also known by their Spanish name, garbanzo beans. They are one of the oldest cultivated legumes. Dried chick-peas need to be soaked in water overnight and cooked in water a long time, up to 3 hours. Canned chick-peas (sometimes sold with the words *ceci cotti,* or "cooked chick peas," on the label) are a convenient alternative to the dried. The taste is identical, so I use them all the time.

Penne with Chick-peas and Mint

Chick-peas and *pasta secca* seasoned with mint bespeaks an antique southern Italian recipe. I've enriched the recipe with more noble vegetables, the artichokes and fennel, and added the blasphemously untraditional cream.

MAKES 2 SERVINGS

———

3 tablespoons extra-virgin olive oil
3 tablespoons finely chopped onion
1/2 cup finely chopped fennel bulb
1 garlic clove, finely chopped
2 cooked artichoke hearts (preferably fresh, although canned or frozen will do), finely chopped
1 cup canned chick-peas, drained
Salt and freshly ground black pepper to taste
1/3 cup dry white wine

3 tablespoons heavy cream (optional)
¹/₂ pound penne rigate
1 tablespoon finely chopped fresh mint leaves
Freshly grated Parmesan cheese

1. Heat the olive oil in a large skillet or casserole over medium-high heat. Cook the onion, fennel, and garlic until sizzling and slightly soft, 3 to 4 minutes, stirring frequently so the garlic doesn't burn. Add the artichokes and chick-peas and continue stirring for 1 to 2 minutes. Season with salt and pepper. Pour in the wine and let it reduce for 4 minutes. Add the cream, if using, and cook until syrupy, about 2 minutes.

2. Meanwhile, bring a large pot of abundantly salted water to a rolling boil and add the penne. Drain when al dente and transfer to the skillet, tossing well so the penne is covered with sauce. Sprinkle with the mint and toss again. Serve with cheese.

Penne Rigate with Fennel and Lemon Zest

This recipe is a more rough-and-ready variation of the previous preparation. Here there is very little prep time and the vegetables are barely cooked. For this reason I think it is a great accompaniment to the equally rustic Grilled Breaded Swordfish (page 211).

MAKES 4 SERVINGS

———

¹/₄ cup extra-virgin olive oil
1 garlic clove, crushed
1 small onion, chopped
1 small fennel bulb, thoroughly washed and chopped
2 teaspoons grated lemon zest
³/₄ pound ripe plum tomatoes, peeled, seeded, and chopped
¹/₂ cup water
Salt and freshly ground black pepper to taste
³/₄ pound penne rigate

———

1. In a large skillet or casserole, heat the olive oil over medium-high heat and cook the garlic clove until it begins to turn light brown, about 1 minute. Remove and discard the garlic. Add the onion, fennel, and lemon zest and cook until soft, about 4 minutes, stirring frequently. Add the tomatoes and water, season with salt and pepper, and cook until the sauce is denser, another 6 minutes, covered, shaking the pan occasionally.

2. Meanwhile, bring a large pot of abundantly salted water to a rolling boil and add the pasta. Drain when al dente, toss with the sauce in the skillet, and serve.

Linguine with Baby Zucchini

This simple recipe is ideal for baby zucchini, which are sweet and delicate. The zucchini should be the size of your thumb. Finding them is the only difficult part to the recipe, and I recommend you cultivate your own zucchini to remedy the problem. Serve with a grilled steak.

MAKES 4 SERVINGS

1/4 cup extra-virgin olive oil
2 garlic cloves, crushed
One 1/4-inch-thick slice pancetta, cut into strips
10 baby zucchini (about 1 pound), sliced
1 tablespoon tomato paste dissolved in 1/4 cup tepid water
Salt and freshly ground black pepper to taste
1 pound linguine
1 cup freshly grated Pecorino cheese

---

1. In a large skillet or casserole, heat the olive oil over medium-high heat and cook the garlic until it begins to turn light brown, about 1 minute. Remove and discard the garlic. Add the pancetta to the skillet and cook for 2 minutes, stirring constantly. Add the zucchini and diluted tomato paste, and cook until the zucchini is soft and the water has evaporated, about 12 minutes, stirring frequently. Reduce the heat if necessary to keep from scorching. Season with salt and pepper.

2. Meanwhile, bring a large pot of abundantly salted water to a rolling boil and add the pasta. Drain when al dente and toss well with the sauce in the skillet. Serve with the cheese on the side.

PECORINO CHEESE

Pecorino is a hard grating cheese made from sheep's milk. The most common type is known as Pecorino Romano, which used to be made in Rome. The ones from Sardinia and Sicily are notable and often available in this country. Pecorino is a sharp-tasting cheese mostly used in lamb cookery and pasta dishes.

In making Pecorino, the cheese maker presses the curd to squeeze all the whey out once it is in the mold. The cheese is dry-salted for about ninety days, pierced in several places so the salt can enter deeper into the cheese, and washed several times. Pecorino Pepato has black peppercorns thrown into the curds and is made often in Sicily. Buy Pecorino by the piece and store it wrapped in plastic in the refrigerator, grating it as needed.

Pine nuts are the seeds of the umbrella pine tree (*Pinus pinea* L.) encased in the pine cone. They are also called by their Italian name *pignoli* (pronounced *pin-NYOL-ee*). They are expensive because of the labor-intensive harvesting process, although Middle Eastern markets sell them for significantly less than supermarkets. Supermarkets usually shelve them in the gourmet foods section, not in the nuts section. Because pine nuts can go rancid, store them in a self-sealing plastic bag in the freezer.

∾

Spaghetti with Spinach, Raisins, and Pine Nuts

If you're familiar with Sicilian food, you'll recognize this combination. For another attractive way of serving, layer the finished spaghetti, without tossing with the bread crumbs, in a baking pan. Sprinkle the bread crumbs on top, drizzle with extra-virgin olive oil, and place in a preheated 425°F oven until the top is a *gratinate*, or golden brown.

MAKES 4 SERVINGS

———

3 tablespoons extra-virgin olive oil
½ red bell pepper, seeded and chopped
1 small onion, finely chopped
2 garlic cloves, finely chopped
3 tablespoons water or dry white wine
1 tablespoon pine nuts
1 tablespoon raisins, soaked in tepid water to cover for 15 minutes
and drained
Pinch of saffron threads
½ teaspoon dried oregano
Salt and freshly ground black pepper to taste
10 ounces fresh spinach, trimmed of tough stems and thoroughly
washed
½ pound spaghetti
2 tablespoons dry bread crumbs

———

1. In a large skillet or casserole, heat the olive oil over medium-high heat and cook the red pepper, onion, and garlic until soft, about 5 minutes, stirring frequently so the garlic doesn't burn. Add the water, pine nuts, raisins, saffron, and oregano and season with salt and pepper. Reduce the heat to medium, add the spinach, and cook another 5 minutes, mixing well. Check the seasonings.

2. Meanwhile, bring a large pot of abundantly salted water to a rolling boil and add the pasta. Drain when al dente and toss with the spinach in the skillet. Dust with the bread crumbs and toss again. Remove to a serving bowl or platter and serve.

~

There are an enormous variety of mushrooms, perhaps up to 40,000, some edible, some poisonous. Unless you are an experienced mushroom forager, buy all your mushrooms at the store. Also, always use fresh mushrooms for recipes, never canned. I remember when the only mushroom available was the common white mushroom (also called the field or button mushroom), a mushroom, incidentally, not much favored by Italians, who prefer wild forest mushrooms over field mushrooms. Today there is a bewildering array of mushrooms available, some in rather odd shapes and colors, including shiitake, cremini, portabella, trumpet, morel, chanterelle, oyster, and enoki. We can now enjoy a selection Italian cooks have had for centuries, and the reason mushroom cookery is so advanced in Italy.

Free-form Lasagne
with Exotic Mushroom Sauce

For a free-form lasagne, the cook uses sheets of lasagne with sauce or other aromatic ingredients as one would any pasta, rather than baking the dish.

Exotic mushrooms started to become less exotic several years ago. Remember that mushroom foraging without the proper training can be dangerous, so always buy your mushrooms at the store. The recipe is easily doubled for more people.

MAKES 2 SERVINGS

———

1 tablespoon extra-virgin olive oil
2 tablespoons unsalted butter
1 garlic clove, crushed
1 ounce fresh white trumpet mushrooms
3 ounces fresh wood ear mushrooms, sliced
1/4 cup dry red wine
2/3 cup veal or chicken broth
1 tablespoon burro mangiatto (see below)
2/3 cup ricotta cheese, preferably fresh
3 tablespoons freshly grated Parmesan cheese
3 tablespoons finely chopped fresh parsley leaves
1/4 pound instant no-boil lasagne (page 87)

———

1. Heat the olive oil with the butter and garlic over medium-high heat in a large skillet or casserole. As the garlic begins to turn light

brown, remove and discard it. Add the mushrooms and cook for 3 minutes, stirring. Pour in the wine and reduce to about 1 tablespoon, about 2 minutes. Add the broth, reduce the heat to low, stir in the burro mangiatto, cover, and simmer until the sauce is unctuous, about 20 minutes. Stir in the ricotta and Parmesan and half the parsley.

2. Meanwhile, bring a large pot of abundantly salted water to a rolling boil, add the lasagne, and cook until al dente, 6 to 7 minutes. Drain well and lay one sheet in a serving casserole. Cover with some of the mushroom sauce and layer another sheet on top. Continue layering until the sauce is used up. Sprinkle the top with the remaining 1½ tablespoons parsley and serve.

NOTE: Burro mangiatto is a sauce thickener made by mashing together 1 tablespoon butter with 1 tablespoon flour.

When buying mushrooms, avoid those that look slimy or bruised. Store them on a less humid shelf of the refrigerator, open to the air inside not in a plastic bag. It is best to clean mushrooms by brushing them with your fingers, a paper towel, or a mushroom brush. Don't wash mushrooms because they absorb water and that will affect the cooking times indicated in the recipe.

Gemelli with Chestnuts and Baby Lima Beans

Gemelli, pasta "twins," are a twisted, short macaroni. They're a little hard to find, so feel free to replace them with similar pasta, such as rotini or fusilli.

Canned chestnuts, which are slightly sweet, and frozen baby lima beans, which hold up well when heated, make this recipe a fast and easy one, but if you can replace both with fresh chestnuts and fresh lima beans the recipe will be even better.

MAKES 4 SERVINGS

One 10-ounce package frozen baby lima beans
³/4 pound gemelli
3 tablespoons extra-virgin olive oil
5 tablespoons finely chopped onion
2 garlic cloves, finely chopped
2 ounces pancetta, chopped
1 tablespoon finely chopped fresh basil or parsley leaves
1 cup chopped canned chestnuts
1 tablespoon tomato paste dissolved in ¹/3 cup water
Salt and freshly ground black pepper to taste
Freshly grated Parmesan cheese to taste
Extra-virgin olive oil

---

1. Bring a large pot of abundantly salted water to a rolling boil for the pasta. Steam the lima beans over the boiling pasta water until

tender. Remove the lima beans and set aside. Put the gemelli in the water and cook. Drain when al dente.

2. Meanwhile, heat the olive oil in a large skillet or casserole over a medium-high heat and cook the soffritto of onion, garlic, pancetta, and basil until soft, about 5 minutes, stirring frequently. Add the chestnuts and cook 1 minute, stirring. Stir the diluted tomato paste into the pan. Cook for 1 minute, then add the reserved lima beans and season with salt and pepper. Add the gemelli, toss well, and serve with cheese and olive oil for drizzling passed around at the table.

Italians traditionally use only four kinds of peppers—bell, peperoncini, cubanelle, and chili peppers. Roasted red bell peppers can be bought loose in Italian markets or jarred. Look for orange bell peppers only for their color; the taste is the same as that of the red bell pepper. Peperoncini are also called Italian long peppers or frying peppers; they are light green and long, with a mild taste. Although Italians use chili peppers, they use them sensibly, avoiding blistering hot preparations.

To peel a pepper, roast it in a preheated 425°F oven until the skin blisters black everywhere, about 40 minutes. Or grill them or hold over a burner until blackened, although this is a little messy, and peel.

Rigatoni with Fried Bell Peppers

The natural sweetness of bell pepper lends this vegetable a property loved by cooks who can combine it with other aromatic ingredients to forge a luscious dish. In this preparation red and yellow peppers make a beautiful contrast over rigatoni.

MAKES 2 SERVINGS

———

1/4 cup extra-virgin olive oil
1 garlic clove, sliced
1 red bell pepper, seeded and sliced into strips
1 yellow bell pepper, seeded and sliced into strips
1/2 teaspoon fennel seeds
1 teaspoon dried oregano
Salt and freshly ground black pepper to taste
1/2 pound rigatoni

———

1. Heat the olive oil in a large skillet or casserole over medium-high heat and cook the garlic and peppers until somewhat softened, about 5 minutes, stirring frequently so the garlic doesn't burn. Reduce the heat to medium, sprinkle over the fennel seeds and oregano, season with salt and pepper, and cook until the peppers are soft, about 15 minutes, stirring occasionally.

2. Meanwhile, bring a large pot of abundantly salted water to a rolling boil and add the pasta. Drain when al dente and toss in the skillet with the pepper mixture. Serve immediately.

Whole Wheat Spaghetti with Quick Pesto Genovese

*W*hole wheat spaghetti gives a rustic taste to many pasta preparations popular in the Veneto region of northern Italy. In this dish it is tossed with pesto, resulting in an attractive combination of pungency and earthiness. Making pesto in a mortar will give you a better result, but takes 10 minutes longer than this method.

MAKES 6 SERVINGS

———

1 bunch fresh basil (50 to 60 medium-size to large leaves), washed and thoroughly dried

2 large garlic cloves, peeled

Pinch of salt

2 tablespoons pine nuts, roasted until golden

3 tablespoons freshly grated Parmesan cheese

3 tablespoons freshly grated Pecorino cheese

1 cup extra-virgin olive oil

1½ pounds whole wheat spaghetti

———

1. Place the basil, garlic, salt, pine nuts, and cheeses in a food processor or blender. Pulse in short bursts until a paste forms. Transfer to a deep bowl and whisk in the olive oil until blended.

2. Meanwhile, bring a large pot of abundantly salted water to a rolling boil and add the pasta. Drain when al dente. Toss the spaghetti with some or all of the pesto and serve immediately.

Basil is an essential herb in Italian cooking, along with parsley and oregano. Only use fresh basil in these recipes. Dried basil loses its taste completely and should not be used. Although some people swear that you can freeze fresh basil, I find the leaves too disgusting looking once they come out of the freezer, although admittedly they maintain their taste pretty well. Personally, my own solution for year-round fresh basil is to keep a basil plant near a sunny spot in my kitchen.

Do not wash or chop basil until you need it.

❧

Linguine Diavolo with Olives and Basil

Large green olives such as the Sicilian Paterno olive or the Cerignola olive can be found in Italian groceries. They are wonderful to nibble on and provide a fresh taste to this delicious pasta preparation with its robust flavors of hot chili peppers, garlic, basil, and anchovy fillets.

MAKES 2 SERVINGS

———

10 large green olives, pitted and chopped
2 garlic cloves, finely chopped
2 tablespoons finely chopped fresh basil leaves
4 salted anchovy fillets, rinsed and patted dry
2 small fresh green chili peppers, seeded and chopped (about 2 tablespoons)
6 tablespoons extra-virgin olive oil
1/2 pound linguine
1 cup freshly grated Pecorino cheese

———

1. Put the olives, garlic, basil, anchovies, peppers, and olive oil in a large skillet or casserole and turn the heat to high. Cook for 2 to 3 minutes, stirring or shaking the casserole frequently. Promptly remove from the burner and set aside until the linguine is cooked.

2. Meanwhile, bring a large pot of abundantly salted water to a rolling boil and add the pasta. Drain when al dente and pour into the skillet. Toss well, then transfer to a serving platter, and toss again with the Pecorino cheese.

Malfadine with Olives and Garlic

*M*alfadine is a curly-edged ribbon of pasta wider than fettuccine. In this recipe the pasta is seasoned with a soffritto of finely chopped olives cooked very quickly with parsley and garlic so that they are heated rather than cooked. This preparation makes a fine first course or accompaniment to Stuffed Squid (page 228).

MAKES 2 SERVINGS

1 cup very finely chopped imported black olives
3 tablespoons extra-virgin olive oil
3 tablespoons finely chopped fresh parsley leaves
1 garlic clove, finely chopped
Salt and freshly ground black pepper to taste
1/2 pound malfadine

1. Put the olives, olive oil, parsley, and garlic in a large skillet or casserole and turn the heat to medium-high. After the soffritto ingredients have been sizzling for 2 minutes, remove from the heat and season with salt and pepper.

2. Meanwhile, bring a large pot of abundantly salted water to a rolling boil and add the pasta. Drain when al dente. Toss the malfadine in the skillet with the olives until the pasta is coated. Serve immediately.

Many medicinal properties are attributed to garlic in Italian family folk remedies. Whether those claims are true or not, garlic is certainly the most important aromatic used in Italian cooking. When buying garlic, avoid those packaged in cellophane wrappers because you will not be able to examine their quality. Look for large, solid cloves without any soft spots. Garlic does not need to be refrigerated; rather, store it in a dark, cool place. An ideal storage container is a small earthenware jar with perforated sides, called a garlic cellar. If your garlic begins to sprout, you will want to remove the bitter-tasting sprout before using.

To peel garlic quickly, place the cloves on a cutting board, lay the flat side of a wide chef's knife on top, and press down until the skin

Capellini with Basil-Garlic Whipped Cream

Capellini, or angel hair pasta, is an extremely delicate strand of pasta that is often ruined by inattentive cooks. It is used with delicate sauces such as in this recipe, where basil, garlic, and whipped cream (whipped to the stiff peak stage) are stirred together, gently heated, and then tossed with the cooked capellini. It's delicious and perfect with a light veal or pork dish.

When cooking capellini, drain it a minute before it reaches the al dente stage because it will continue to cook while you are tossing it with the sauce.

MAKES 4 SERVINGS

———

10 large fresh basil leaves, finely chopped
3 garlic cloves, finely chopped
1¹/₂ cups whipped cream
2 tablespoons extra-virgin olive oil
1 pound capellini
Freshly ground black pepper to taste

———

1. In a large skillet or casserole, heat the basil, garlic, whipped cream, and olive oil over medium heat for 2 minutes. Turn the heat off, but keep warm.

2. Meanwhile, bring a large pot of abundantly salted water to a rolling boil and add the pasta. Drain just short of al dente. Add the drained pasta to the skillet with a sprinkling of pepper. Toss well, cook for 2 minutes over low heat, and serve.

Fried Tortellini

This is so easy and quick. I made it one afternoon when I realized I had to leave the house in fifteen minutes but wanted a non–fast-food bite to eat. The real surprise was how good it was.

MAKES 1 SERVING

———

¹/₄ cup extra-virgin olive oil
¹/₄ pound fresh tortellini, your choice of stuffing
Freshly grated Parmesan cheese

———

1. Heat the olive oil in a small skillet until nearly smoking over medium-high heat. Cook the tortellini until golden brown, about 5 minutes, shaking and tossing the pan so all the sides are browned evenly.

2. Remove from the skillet with a slotted ladle to a pasta bowl, leaving the oil behind. Sprinkle with cheese and serve.

cracks. Remove the skin and chop. Some people like to use garlic presses, but I don't care for them; the garlic comes out too mushy and the press then needs to be cleaned.

Powdered, dried, and salted garlic are not used in Italian cooking.

~

Mascarpone is a soft, creamy fresh cheese with a buttery flavor originally produced in Lombardy. Today, there are many domestic producers with excellent mascarpone products. Mascarpone is made by curdling fresh cow's milk cream with citric acid, producing a final product that looks like very thick cream. The fat content is high, and mascarpone is typically used in desserts or pasta dishes in place of butter or cream.

~

Cavatelli with Creamy Cheese Fondue

Cavatelli are special little pastas popular in southern Italy and Sicily. They are, essentially, orecchiette that have been rolled up. In the Francis Ford Coppola movie *Godfather III*, there is one erotic scene where the Corleone cousins make cavatelli in a slow, methodical way that is also gastronomically instructive.

In this preparation the various cheeses are blended in a double boiler for a satisfying dinner.

MAKES 4 SERVINGS

———

$^1/_2$ *pound ricotta cheese*
$^1/_2$ *cup mascarpone cheese*
$^1/_4$ *pound fresh mozzarella cheese, diced*
$^1/_4$ *cup freshly grated Pecorino cheese*
2 slices prosciutto, chopped
1 tablespoon extra-virgin olive oil
2 tablespoons heavy cream
3 tablespoons dry Marsala wine
Salt and freshly ground black pepper to taste
1 pound cavatelli

———

1. Bring some water to a simmer in the bottom of a double boiler. In the top part of the double boiler, melt and combine the ricotta, mascarpone, mozzarella, and Pecorino with the prosciutto, olive oil, cream, Marsala, salt, and pepper, stirring in a figure-eight motion.

2. Meanwhile, bring a large pot of abundantly salted water to a rolling boil and add the pasta. Drain when al dente and place in a

serving bowl. Once the cheeses have melted and blended, pour the mixture over the pasta and toss with more Pecorino to taste until evenly coated.

Fettuccine with Mascarpone Sauce

This delightfully simple preparation is creamy and cheesy and delicious. Save the egg whites to make Floating Islands in a Raspberry Sea (page 264) after dinner.

MAKES 4 SERVINGS

———

2 large egg yolks
3 tablespoons extra-virgin olive oil
1/2 cup mascarpone cheese
Salt and freshly ground black pepper to taste
3/4 pound fresh fettuccine
1/2 cup freshly grated Parmesan cheese

———

1. Place the egg yolks in a small mixing bowl and slowly beat in the olive oil in a very thin stream, beating all the time, as you would for making a mayonnaise. Add the mascarpone a little at a time and season with salt and pepper.

2. Bring a large pot of abundantly salted water to a rolling boil. Drop the pasta in gradually. Drain when al dente and transfer to a serving bowl or platter and cover with the sauce. Toss well and sprinkle with Parmesan. Serve immediately.

THE RISK OF SALMONELLA

Egg-borne salmonella poisoning received a lot of press in the 1980s. The threat is, for the most part, exaggerated and misplaced. Salmonella poisoning can occur in *all* foods that are improperly handled, usually by being held at incorrect temperatures or through cross-contamination. The USDA reports that one in every 10,000 raw eggs is contaminated with some salmonella bacteria (it requires millions to cause sickness). Salmonella poisoning is rarely fatal; the usual symptoms are nausea, vomiting, and diarrhea not requiring treatment. People at risk, such as the elderly, the very young, pregnant women, and people with weakened immune systems should exercise the same caution they use with other foods. Practice standard kitchen hygiene and you need not be afraid of raw eggs.

Taleggio is a dry-salted
whole cow's milk cheese
from Lombardy. It is a soft,
fat cheese that is ripe after
two months. The creaminess
of this cheese contributes to
its popularity. It is usually
surrounded by a white paraf-
fin coating and a moldy rind
with a light yellow cheese.
Best served at room temperature as a table cheese,
Taleggio is also a good melting cheese for some recipes.
It is sold in Italian markets
and supermarkets with good
cheese departments.

∽

Spaghetti with Six Cheeses

Since you may not find the cheeses I call for in this recipe, just remember that some should be mild and soft and the others should be strong like a blue cheese. Use only cow's cheese. The flavors of this dish are wonderfully perfumed. Because there is so much cheese, you will want to follow this pasta with a light salad or a very simple white meat, such as chicken breast, grilled or pan seared.

MAKES 4 TO 6 SERVINGS

———

2 tablespoons unsalted butter
1 tablespoon extra-virgin olive oil
3/4 cup chopped pancetta (about 2 ounces)
2 ounces Taleggio cheese, diced
2 ounces Bel Paese cheese, diced
2 ounces Gorgonzola cheese, crumbled
2 ounces Fontina cheese, diced
2 ounces mascarpone cheese
2 ounces smoked (preferably) or regular ricotta cheese, diced
3/4 cup sparkling white wine (such as Asti Spumante)
1 garlic clove, crushed
Freshly ground white pepper to taste
1 pound spaghetti
1 tablespoon finely chopped fresh parsley leaves

———

1. Melt the butter in a large skillet or casserole over medium heat, then add the olive oil and pancetta and cook the pancetta until it

begins to brown, about 5 minutes. Take the pan off the heat and remove and discard all but 1 tablespoon of the cooking fats.

2. Add the cheeses, wine, garlic, and pepper and stir in a figure-eight motion over medium heat until all the cheeses have melted and are smooth. Cook until it begins to bubble slightly. If the cheese is already bubbling too much, reduce the heat till it stops.

3. Meanwhile, bring a large pot of abundantly salted water to a rolling boil and add the pasta. Drain when al dente. Transfer the spaghetti to the skillet and toss, then remove to a serving platter and sprinkle with the parsley.

∾

Bel Paese is a semi-soft cheese ripened by mold or yeast present on its surface. It is imported, sometimes wrapped in foil, and can be found in Italian markets and increasingly in supermarkets. Bel Paese makes a good table cheese, too. Its flavor is mild and the closer to room temperature, the better.

∾

CHAPTER FIVE

Pasta with Meat

YEARS AGO, WHEN Italian families were much poorer, meat was expensive, used as a condiment to flavor bowls of durum-wheat macaroni. Today the Italians are among the most sophisticated, technologically advanced, and well-off peoples of Europe and, indeed, the industrialized western world. In the kitchen, that means meat portions become bigger and appear more often. But I love the traditional Italian family's approach to meat: used in small portions as a flavoring for pasta. These recipes use products such as the lusty-tasting pancetta, a cured pork belly often described as Italian bacon or good-quality Italian sausage. Remember that the idea is to give the pasta flavor, so you can, if you desire, use even less meat than I call for in the recipes.

Pancetta (pronounced *pan-CHETT-a*) is a cured Italian bacon found in Italian markets and occasionally in well-stocked supermarket delis. Its flavor is quite different from that of American bacon, which is a salt-cured and smoked pork belly, while pancetta is a salt- or air-cured and unsmoked product that goes through a more delicate maturing process. If you can't find pancetta, use sliced slab bacon that has been blanched in boiling water for three to five minutes.

∾

Whole Wheat Spaghetti with Pancetta

I sometimes find it hard to convince people that simple recipes, like this one, are often my favorites. In this preparation the earthy taste of whole wheat spaghetti is enhanced by the equally pastoral tastes of pancetta and pork lard, used simply as flavor embellishments. Make this recipe once and it will become part of your standard repertoire.

MAKES 4 SERVINGS

———

1 tablespoon pork lard
2 tablespoons extra-virgin olive oil
2 ounces pancetta, cut into thin strips
1/4 cup finely chopped fresh parsley leaves
1 large garlic clove, finely chopped
3/4 pound whole wheat spaghetti
1/2 cup freshly grated Pecorino cheese, or to taste
Freshly ground black pepper to taste

———

1. In a large skillet or casserole, melt the lard with the olive oil over medium-high heat. Add the pancetta and cook until some fat is rendered, about 4 minutes, stirring frequently. Add the parsley and garlic, stirring for 1 minute. Remove the pan from the heat.

2. Meanwhile, bring a large pot of abundantly salted water to a rolling boil and add the pasta. Drain when al dente. Toss the pasta with the sauce in the skillet. Toss again with the cheese and pepper. Serve immediately.

Lasagnette with Pancetta and White Onions

Lasagnette is a flat pasta about ¾ inch wide usually sold in well-stocked supermarkets and always in a good Italian grocery. This is an easy preparation in which the onion is cooked with the pancetta until golden and then tossed with the pasta. This family recipe is a specialty of the villages of the Apennines near Bologna, in Emilia-Romagna.

MAKES 4 TO 6 SERVINGS

———

3 tablespoons extra-virgin olive oil
½ pound pancetta, finely diced
1½ pounds white onions, peeled and thinly sliced
¾ cup water
Salt and freshly ground black pepper to taste
¾ pound lasagnette
Freshly grated Parmesan cheese (optional) to taste

———

1. Heat the olive oil in a large skillet or casserole over medium heat and brown the pancetta for 10 minutes, stirring occasionally. Add the onions and water, season with salt and pepper, and cook until the onions are soft, stirring often, for another 15 minutes.

2. Meanwhile, bring a large pot of abundantly salted water to a rolling boil and add the pasta. Drain when al dente. Transfer the pasta to a serving platter or bowl, toss with the onion sauce, and serve immediately with Parmesan cheese if desired.

Spaghetti with Pancetta

*C*rispy cooked pancetta has that rustic taste that some Italian food writers call Homeric. Tossed with the equally rustic Pecorino, it is a very satisfying first course and gets a nice bite from the red pepper. I usually follow this dish, or accompany it, with fish.

MAKES 4 SERVINGS

---

3 tablespoons extra-virgin olive oil
1 tablespoon lard
¹/₄ pound pancetta, chopped
2 dried red chili peppers
1 small onion, peeled
1 garlic clove, peeled
Pinch of salt
1 pound spaghetti
3 ounces Pecorino cheese, grated

---

1. In a large skillet or casserole, heat the olive oil with the lard over medium heat and cook the pancetta and chili peppers, stirring, until the pancetta is yellowed and some fat rendered, about 5 minutes. Remove the pancetta to a platter with a slotted ladle.

2. Chop the onion and garlic together and add to the skillet with the salt. Cook until the onion is translucent, 6 to 7 minutes, stirring. Return the pancetta to the skillet and heat through.

3. Meanwhile, bring a large pot of abundantly salted water to a rolling boil and add the pasta. Drain when al dente. Transfer the spaghetti to a serving platter. Immediately cover with the cheese and

then the pancetta-and-onion soffritto. Toss this mixture at tableside and serve, being careful you don't eat the red peppers if you have not already removed them.

Spaghetti with Pancetta and Tomatoes

Que sapore! What a flavor! This preparation has a wonderful aroma, as the Italians say. The soffritto of pancetta, onion, garlic, and parsley gives an aromatic depth to the lusciously melting tomatoes.

MAKES 4 SERVINGS

3 tablespoons extra-virgin olive oil
1 garlic clove, very finely chopped
1 small onion, very finely chopped
1 teaspoon very finely chopped fresh parsley leaves
1/4 pound pancetta, chopped or cut into thin strips
8 very ripe plum tomatoes (about 1 pound), peeled, seeded, and finely chopped
2 tablespoons dry red wine
2 tablespoons water
1 tablespoon very finely chopped fresh basil leaves
Freshly ground black pepper to taste
1 pound spaghetti
Freshly grated Parmesan cheese to taste

1. In a large skillet or casserole, heat the olive oil over medium-high heat and cook the garlic, onion, parsley, and pancetta until the onion is soft, about 4 minutes, stirring occasionally. Add the tomatoes,

wine, water, basil, and pepper and cook until dense, another 8 minutes. If the sauce is drying out, add another tablespoon of water and cook until the sauce is a little thicker, about 2 more minutes.

2. Meanwhile, bring a large pot of abundantly salted water to a rolling boil and add the pasta. Drain when al dente. Toss well with the sauce in the skillet and serve with abundant cheese.

Fettuccine Fresca with Pancetta

This is so easy that there is a temptation to start adding more ingredients—don't. Do it this way and you will be very happy. Buy the best-quality, locally made fresh fettuccine or make your own.

MAKES 4 SERVINGS

1/4 cup extra-virgin olive oil
1/4 pound pancetta, thinly sliced
2 garlic cloves, finely chopped
1 pound fresh fettuccine
1 to 1 1/2 cups freshly grated Pecorino cheese
Freshly ground black pepper to taste

----

1. Heat the olive oil in a large skillet or casserole and cook the pancetta, stirring, over high heat until crisp but not dark brown, about 4 minutes. Remove the skillet from the heat and add the garlic.

2. Meanwhile, bring a large pot of abundantly salted water to a rolling boil, and add the pasta. Drain when al dente. Add the pasta to the skillet and toss with the pancetta and cheese until evenly coated. Serve with freshly ground black pepper.

A well-stocked Italian market will have a delightful array of hanging dried *salame*. There should be Genoa, Milano, and Napolitana, plus, sopresatta, capicolla, coppa, prosciutto, porchetta, mortadella, and perhaps rarer ones such as soppresa Veneta.

American supermarket delis also sell salami, but generally they buy the products of large manufacturers, which I think are inferior to the salamis made by small producers or individuals in the area. You would be amazed at the number of people of Italian extraction in this country who make their own salami. Look for these usually small Italian groceries in your surrounding neighborhoods: they're everywhere in this country.

Rigatoni with Soppresa Veneta

Soppresa Veneta is a flavorful soft pork salami made in Venice. It is not imported, but domestic brands are available that are just fine. It is quite mild and if an Italian deli doesn't carry it, ask for Milano or Genoa salami. This recipe is a variation, more or less, of Spaghetti with Fennel (page 53), with a few extra touches.

MAKES 4 SERVINGS

¼ cup extra-virgin olive oil
1 cup very finely chopped onion
2 garlic cloves, very finely chopped
1 cup very finely chopped fennel bulb
6 to 8 very ripe plum tomatoes (about ¾ pound), peeled, seeded, and chopped
¼ pound sliced salami, chopped
¼ cup dry red wine
Salt and freshly ground black pepper to taste
¾ pound rigatoni
Freshly grated Parmesan cheese to taste

1. In a large skillet or casserole, heat the olive oil over medium heat and cook the onion, garlic, and fennel until soft, about 6 minutes, stirring frequently. Add the tomatoes, salami, and wine, season with salt and pepper, and cook until most of the water from the tomatoes has evaporated, about 10 minutes.

2. Meanwhile, bring a large pot of abundantly salted water to a rolling boil and add the pasta. Drain when al dente and toss with the sauce in the skillet. Serve with cheese.

Free-form Lasagne
with Olive and Pancetta Sauce

This free-form lasagne is seasoned with good-quality imported olives and the earthy taste of pancetta. The best lasagne noodles to use for this preparation is the ultra-thin "no-boil" type. Of course, you have to boil them for this recipe—six to seven minutes—while you prepare the sauce, but you will find this variety much better than the thicker lasagne noodles you've used in the past.

MAKES 2 SERVINGS

———

2 tablespoons extra-virgin olive oil
2 ounces pancetta, chopped
2 or 3 garlic cloves, finely chopped
3 tablespoons finely chopped fresh parsley leaves
1/3 cup dry white wine
1/3 cup chopped imported green olives
Freshly ground black pepper to taste
1/2 pound instant no-boil lasagne noodles
1/2 cup freshly grated Parmesan cheese

———

1. Heat the olive oil with the pancetta in a large skillet or casserole over medium-high heat until crispy, about 6 minutes, stirring. Reduce the heat to medium and add the garlic and parsley, stirring constantly for 1 minute. Pour in the wine and olives and cook until the wine is reduced, about 4 minutes. Season with pepper.

continued

2. Meanwhile, bring a large pot of abundantly salted water to a rolling boil and add the lasagne noodles, one sheet at a time. Drain when al dente. Toss the noodles with the sauce in the skillet. Toss again with the cheese. Serve immediately.

Mezze Ziti with Pancetta, Prosciutto, Pistachios, and Peas

A mellow preparation that delivers an unpretentious flavor. Remember not to salt anything: there's already enough salt from the cured meats. I use various cold cuts, or *salume*, in this recipe, including the cured meat sausage known as coppa. Coppa is a popular Italian cured meat made from pork loin and neck that is moist, tender, and lean. Because coppa is so lean, it can become stringy if left out in the air too long, so Italian families often wrap their homemade coppa in a wine-soaked cheesecloth, which not only keeps it damp but adds another level of flavor.

MAKES 4 TO 6 SERVINGS

———

3 tablespoons extra-virgin olive oil
1 tablespoon lard
1 medium-size onion, chopped
3 garlic cloves, finely chopped
Two ¼-inch-thick slices pancetta (about ¼ pound),
cut into long, thin strips
Two ¼-inch-thick slices prosciutto (about ¼ pound),
cut into long, thin strips

Pistachios are not often associated with Italian cooking, but in Sicily they are a popular nut found not only in sweets but also in cooked dishes, a legacy of Sicily's medieval Arab era. Buy only imported green pistachios; never use those that have been dyed red. Middle Eastern markets usually sell shelled nuts. Store them in the freezer, since nuts turn rancid.

∾

Two ¹/₄-inch-thick slices coppa (about ¹/₄ pound),
cut into long, thin strips
¹/₂ cup shelled raw pistachios
1 teaspoon dried oregano
Freshly ground black pepper to taste
3 tablespoons water
1 pound mezze ziti (cut or uncut)
1 cup frozen peas
2 ounces hard ricotta salata cheese, grated

———

1. Heat the olive oil and lard together in a large skillet or casserole over medium-high heat and cook the onion, garlic, and pancetta until the onion is soft, about 5 minutes, stirring or shaking occasionally. Add the prosciutto, coppa, pistachios, oregano, and pepper and stir again. Cook for 2 to 3 minutes, then remove the sauce to a platter. Pour the water into the skillet and scrape the bottom so all the browned bits dissolve into it. Return the sauce to the skillet.

2. Meanwhile, bring a large pot of abundantly salted water to a rolling boil and add the pasta. About 5 minutes before the pasta reaches al dente, add the peas. Drain when pasta is al dente. Transfer the pasta and peas to the skillet, toss with the sauce and ricotta salata, and serve.

Spaghetti with Cooked and Cured Ham

The prosciutto made in the province of Parma in Italy is considered the world's finest cured ham product. The meat from the finest pigs are cured without the use of any artificial preservatives. Once the ham is salted, the curing process lasts up to a year, carefully controlled. A law stipulates the exact regions that are allowed to use the name *prosciutto di Parma*. Even the kind of pig to be used and how it should be raised before slaughter are regulated. All this creates a prosciutto absolutely extraordinary in taste. The ham melts in your mouth.

Save the expensive prosciutto di Parma for antipasti and uncooked dishes, and make sure the person slicing it is either Italian or knows that the prosciutto must be sliced so thin as to be translucent—and don't let him tell you it can't be done. If the ham is

In Italy, what we call boiled ham is called *prosciutto cotto* and what we call prosciutto is *prosciutto crudo*. When you're in a *salumeria* (delicatessen) in Italy, you will need to specify.

This is a mild yet flavorful pasta dish, ideal for young palates. The prosciutto gives the spaghetti extra flavor to make it interesting.

MAKES 4 SERVINGS

————

1/4 cup extra-virgin olive oil or unsalted butter, or a combination of both
2 small zucchini, peeled and chopped
2 ounces prosciutto, sliced and chopped
2 ounces boiled ham, sliced and chopped
1/2 teaspoon fresh or dried thyme
1 pound spaghetti
Freshly grated Parmesan cheese to taste

————

1. In a large skillet or casserole, heat the olive oil and/or melt the butter over medium heat. When the bubbling butter (if using) subsides, add the zucchini and cook, stirring, until coated with olive oil and softening, 3 to 4 minutes. Add the prosciutto and ham, and cook until both begin to curl, another 3 minutes, stirring. Sprinkle with the thyme, stir, and set aside.

2. Meanwhile, bring a large pot of abundantly salted water to a rolling boil and add the pasta. Drain when al dente and toss with the sauce in the skillet. Serve immediately with cheese.

Fettuccine with Ham and
Warm Goat Cheese

It was a cold night when I first made this dish. I wanted to satisfy three conditions. First, the dish had to be quick and easy to prepare; second, it had to have mellow flavors; and third, I didn't want the tastes too robust, just enough for a cozy, filling feeling. This was the result.

MAKES 2 SERVINGS

———

1/2 pound fettuccine
1/4 pound sliced cooked ham, cut into short, thin strips
2 ounces soft goat cheese, crumbled
2 tablespoons chopped roasted red bell pepper
1 garlic clove, very finely chopped
1 tablespoon very finely chopped fresh parsley leaves
Extra-virgin olive oil to taste
Freshly ground black pepper to taste

———

1. Bring a large pot of abundantly salted water to a rolling boil and add the pasta. Drain when al dente.

2. Toss the pasta with the ham, goat cheese, roasted red pepper, garlic, parsley, and olive oil in a large serving bowl. Sprinkle some black pepper over the top and serve.

shredding while being sliced, pass it by because it means the prosciutto has dried out from mishandling. For cooking and eating purposes, the domestic prosciutto made by the San Daniele or Citterio firms is excellent. In Italy every region has its own prosciutto. When I visit my relatives in Italy, they always serve their family-made prosciutto. Incidentally, you may hear some people call prosciutto *prosciut.* This is a rough dialectal way of saying it in southern Italy and some Americans have curiously picked it up.

◦

A very nice addition to many prepared dishes is a light drizzle of red pepper olive oil. To make it, remove about ½ cup oil from any bottle of olive oil and replace it with as many dried red chili peppers as you can fit in. Cap the bottle and let sit in a cool, dark place for two weeks before using. Use the oil within six months (to avoid bacterial development owing to the chili peppers).

~

Penne with Roasted Chestnuts and Grilled Sausage

This preparation is strictly a leftovers meal. Although you could use fresh sausages and canned chestnuts, the dish will not be the same because canned chestnuts are too sweet, changing the nature of this dish entirely. The lingering aroma of the grill and the roasted chestnuts is what makes the combination so robust. It is substantial enough that I would not serve anything but a simple green vegetable along with it.

MAKES 2 SERVINGS

———

3 tablespoons extra-virgin olive oil
2 ounces pancetta, ripped into pieces
3 tablespoons finely chopped fresh parsley leaves
2 garlic cloves, finely chopped
½ pound leftover grilled sausage, about 2 links, sliced (see note below)
20 roasted chestnuts, peeled and chopped
Salt and freshly ground black pepper to taste
½ cup dry white wine
½ pound penne
½ cup freshly grated Parmesan cheese
Red pepper olive oil (optional)

———

1. Heat the olive oil in a skillet or casserole large enough to hold all the pasta over medium-high heat and cook the pancetta until it siz-

zles, about 1 minute. Add the parsley and garlic, cooking for 30 seconds while stirring constantly. Add the sausage and chestnuts, and cook until heated through, about 5 minutes. Season with salt and pepper. Pour in the wine and cook until it evaporates, about 5 minutes.

2. Meanwhile, bring a large pot of abundantly salted water to a rolling boil and add the pasta. Drain the pasta when al dente and add to the sauce in the skillet. Mix well. Add the cheese and toss. Serve immediately with red pepper oil if desired.

NOTE: If using fresh sausages, remove the meat from the casings and cook in a skillet over medium heat until it loses its pinkness, about 15 minutes, adding small amounts of water so it doesn't stick. Remove with a slotted spoon.

In the Middle Ages, some northern Italian families virtually lived on chestnuts, especially during times of famine. Chestnut flour was made into what people called "tree bread." Roasted chestnuts are an old favorite in Italy as much as in America; in fact, Pliny in his *Natural History* tells us that the Romans only ate them roasted.

To roast chestnuts, carefully (so you don't cut yourself) make an "X" on their convex side with a small paring knife and place in a roasting pan in a preheated 400°F oven for 40 minutes. Remove the shell and continue with the preparation or reserve for another use.

An Italian family cook frequently cooks with wine. I remember my mom always kept a jug of Chianti in the refrigerator that she used both for cooking, especially in her ragùs, and for drinking, usually in a jelly jar type of glass. Remember the scene in the first *Godfather* movie, when Pauli tells the young Michael Corleone (Al Pacino) that he should know how to make a good sauce in case he has to cook for a bunch of guys some day? In go the tomatoes, tomato paste, sugar, meatballs, sausages, and, Pauli explains, "a little wine."

An inexpensive but robust red wine, such as Chianti or Montepulciano, and a white, such as Fontina Candida or Corvo, are perfect for cooking purposes. Marsala is a sweet or dry fortified Sicilian wine used in some recipes. Asti Spumante is a sparkling

Penne Rigate with Sausage and Pepper Sauce

Penne rigate is a quill-shaped pasta with ridges, ideally suited to this spicy hot sausage and pepper sauce. Although cherry tomatoes are most often used in salads, their color and shape are so appetizing that I use them here.

MAKES 2 TO 3 SERVINGS

———

¼ cup extra-virgin olive oil
1 green bell pepper, seeded and chopped
1 small onion, chopped
3 garlic cloves, finely chopped
2 mild Italian sausage links, casings removed and chopped
¼ pound cooked ham, sliced and chopped
2 cups cherry tomatoes, cut in half and seeded
1 cup dry red wine
Pinch of cayenne pepper, or to taste
Freshly ground black pepper to taste
½ pound penne rigate
Freshly grated Parmesan cheese to taste

———

1. Heat the olive oil in a large skillet or casserole over medium-high heat and cook the green pepper, onion, and garlic until a little soft, about 4 minutes, stirring frequently so the garlic doesn't burn. Add the sausage, ham, and tomatoes and cook until the sausage meat has lost its pink and the tomatoes are soft, about 6 minutes, stirring occasionally. Pour in the wine and stir, then sprinkle on the cayenne and

black pepper. Stir again, cover, and cook until thick, about 20 minutes. Turn off the heat.

2. Meanwhile, bring a large pot of abundantly salted water to a rolling boil and add the pasta. Drain when al dente and toss with the sauce in the skillet. Serve with cheese.

wine that can be used in recipes calling for sparkling wine. Some Italian cookbook writers say you should cook with the same wine you would drink. I agree, but only if the wine you are drinking is good and inexpensive. You would be crazy to cook with expensive wine.

Perciatelli with Sausages and Olives

*O*ne day some years ago my friends David Forbes and Ginny Sherwood threw a big party and decided to make a recipe they had fallen in love with from my book *Lasagne* (Little, Brown, 1995). As a cookbook writer, I was pleased that they had decided to cook rather than cater the party, and I agreed to help them the night before.

The lasagne they chose is called *lasagne alla Catanese* and is made with fried eggplant, olives, garlic, tomatoes, yellow bell peppers, anchovies, capers, and mozzarella cheese. But we had to make enough for seventy people. We bought too many olives and too much sausage for another dish, and since we couldn't eat the lasagne that was reserved for the party, I made them this recipe, which we all loved.

MAKES 4 TO 6 SERVINGS

———

2 pounds mild Italian sausages
1 pound perciatelli
1 cup chopped imported green olives
1/4 cup extra-virgin olive oil
1/2 cup freshly grated Pecorino or Parmesan cheese
Freshly ground black pepper to taste
Cayenne pepper (optional) to taste
Finely chopped fresh parsley leaves (optional)

———

1. Put the sausages in a saucepan and cover with cold water. Bring to a boil. When the water starts bubbling, reduce the heat to medium

and cook until all pinkness is gone, about 30 minutes. Drain the sausages, pat dry, and set aside.

2. Meanwhile, bring a large pot of abundantly salted water to a rolling boil and add the pasta. Drain when al dente. Transfer the pasta to a large serving bowl, toss with the olives, olive oil, and cheese, and season with black pepper. Arrange the sausages on top and serve with a sprinkling of cayenne pepper and chopped parsley, if desired.

Spaghetti with Sausage and Ricotta Sauce

Although I often make my own Italian sausages, I also rely heavily on store-bought, though they can be a dicey affair. I've had everything from ghastly supermarket-made Italian sausages that were literally inedible to wonderful, juicy, full-flavored ones. Just remember (if you're not inclined to make your own) that those good sausages are out there—you just need to shop around.

This quick and filling dish can be spiced up, if you want, with some red pepper. Use lots of parsley, definitely.

MAKES 4 SERVINGS

———

1/2 pound mild Italian sausages, casings removed and crumbled
3/4 cup water
2 tablespoons unsalted butter
2 tablespoons extra-virgin olive oil
2 salted anchovy fillets, rinsed and patted dry
1 garlic clove, finely chopped
1/4 cup finely chopped fresh parsley leaves
1 pound ricotta cheese, preferably fresh
1/4 cup freshly grated Parmesan cheese
Salt and freshly ground black pepper to taste
1/4 teaspoon red chili pepper flakes (optional)
3/4 pound spaghetti

———

1. In a medium-size skillet or casserole, cook the crumbled sausage over medium-high heat with 1/4 cup of the water until it loses its

pinkness, about 5 minutes. Remove with a slotted spoon, pressing any fat out with the back of a wooden spoon. Set aside.

2. In the same skillet you cooked the sausage, melt the butter with the olive oil over medium heat. Add the anchovies, garlic, and parsley and cook for 1 minute, stirring constantly. Add the cheeses and remaining ½ cup water, and season with salt and black and red pepper flakes, if using. Stir to blend and leave over medium heat until the pasta is ready.

3. Meanwhile, bring a large pot of abundantly salted water to a rolling boil and add the pasta. Drain when al dente, toss with the sauce in the skillet, and serve.

Spaghetti with Sausage, Tomato, and Ricotta Sauce

This recipe is a variation on the previous recipe. Here the aromatic tastes are more powerful, the soffritto of onions, garlic, mint, and parsley (which you can chop together) providing an exciting spike to the sausages in tomatoes.

MAKES 4 SERVINGS

1/4 cup extra-virgin olive oil

1 pound mild Italian sausages, casings removed and crumbled

One 16-ounce can whole plum tomatoes, chopped

1/4 cup finely chopped onion

1 garlic clove, finely chopped

1 tablespoon freshly squeezed lemon juice

1 tablespoon finely chopped fresh mint leaves

1 tablespoon finely chopped fresh parsley leaves

1 teaspoon dried oregano

1/2 cup hot water

Salt and freshly ground black pepper to taste

1/2 pound ricotta cheese (mashed if fresh)

3/4 pound spaghetti

Freshly grated Pecorino cheese to taste

---

1. In a large skillet or casserole, heat the olive oil over medium-high heat, add the sausages, tomatoes, onion, garlic, lemon juice, mint,

parsley, oregano, and water, and season with salt and pepper. Reduce the heat to medium and cook until the sauce is dense, about 20 minutes, stirring occasionally. Stir in the ricotta and remove from the heat.

2. Meanwhile, bring a large pot of abundantly salted water to a rolling boil and add the pasta. Drain when al dente and toss with the sauce in the skillet. Serve with cheese.

Zucchini are annual plants that grow quite large, spreading their huge leaves and bright yellow flowers four feet from the plant's center. Growing your own zucchini plants is worth the effort for a number of reasons. As do Italian families, you will be able to pick zucchini far younger than any you will see at a market, and these baby zucchini are sweeter and far more flavorful. You can also pick the baby zucchini with their flowers attached.

In the spring, buy your zucchini plants or seeds from a local garden store and plant them in a sunny portion of your garden or in large flower pots. All the zucchini need is some water and some sun, and by early August you can start harvesting.

Tubetti with Sausage and Zucchini Blossoms

*W*hen are American markets going to sell baby zucchini with their blossoms attached as they do in little markets around Italy? At the very least, the farmer's markets around the country should be doing it as they do in California. So if your local farmer's market doesn't, you'll have to plant your own zucchini.

This flavorful pasta dish can be eaten with a spoon. It has just the right degree of hotness and is a colorful kelly green because of the zucchini mixed with their yellow flowers.

MAKES 2 TO 3 SERVINGS

———

1/2 pound mild Italian sausages, casings removed and crumbled
3 tablespoons extra-virgin olive oil
1/4 cup finely chopped onion
1 garlic clove, finely chopped
1 fresh green chili pepper, about 4 inches long, seeded and finely chopped
3 baby zucchini with their blossoms, chopped
1/4 teaspoon red chili pepper flakes
Salt and freshly ground black pepper to taste
1/2 cup dry white wine
1/2 pound tubetti
1/2 cup freshly grated Parmesan cheese

———

1. In a medium-size skillet or casserole, cook the sausage meat over medium heat until it loses its pinkness, 5 to 6 minutes. Remove with

a slotted spoon, squeezing out any fat with the back of a wooden spoon, and set aside.

2. In a large skillet or casserole, heat the olive oil and cook the onion, garlic, and chili pepper, stirring, over medium heat until soft, about 4 minutes. Add the zucchini and blossoms and the red pepper flakes, season with salt and black pepper, and cook for 2 minutes. Pour in the wine and reduce by half. Add the sausage to the sauce.

3. Meanwhile, bring a large pot of abundantly salted water to a rolling boil and add the pasta. Drain when al dente and toss with the sauce in the skillet. Sprinkle on the cheese, toss again, and serve.

If you're not growing your own zucchini, shop for the smallest ones possible. When zucchini get big, they become woody and their natural sweetness disappears.

Fettuccine with Rib Eye Steak
and Spinach

This is a "no-nonsense" preparation. The tastes are so satisfying, *and* you get your meat fix, your vegetable, and your carbohydrate. This preparation is suited to leftover spinach, though the recipe cooks fresh spinach quickly and easily before the steaks. Make it as hot as you want or let your family sprinkle on the cayenne pepper at the table, along with the Parmesan cheese. You can also reduce the butter and olive oil by half without affecting the recipe in any major way.

MAKES 4 SERVINGS

———

2 tablespoons unsalted butter
1/4 cup extra-virgin olive oil
2 garlic cloves, finely chopped
10 ounces fresh spinach, trimmed of tough stems and
thoroughly washed
Four 1/4-inch-thick rib eye steaks (about 1 pound), trimmed of fat
Cayenne pepper to taste
Salt and freshly ground black pepper to taste
3/4 pound fettuccine
1/2 cup freshly grated Parmesan cheese

———

1. Heat the butter, 2 tablespoons of the olive oil, and the garlic in a large skillet or casserole over medium-high heat, add the spinach, and cook until it wilts. Remove the spinach and set aside.

2. Sprinkle the steaks with the cayenne, salt, and black pepper. Add the remaining 2 tablespoons olive oil to the skillet and cook the steaks until brown, about 4 minutes per side. Return the spinach to the pan and cook until reheated, about 1 minute.

3. Meanwhile, bring a large pot of abundantly salted water to a rolling boil and add the pasta. Drain when al dente. Transfer the pasta to a serving platter and sprinkle on ¼ cup of the cheese. Cover with the steak, spinach, and the remaining ¼ cup cheese and serve.

Italians are quite fond of this noble vegetable. The flesh at the bottom of the inside of the bracts (*not* properly called leaves) is edible, as is the foundation, or heart. Buy artichokes that feel heavy with closed bracts. If the leaves have begun to spread, the artichoke is not of the highest quality. Look at the stem for small holes that might indicate worm damage and pass those by. Black spots on artichokes are only the result of frost damage; they are otherwise fine. The most common one on the market is the globe artichoke. A specialty greengrocer might carry the violet Tuscany artichoke, which tapers off at the top into a beautiful purple tip.

Fresh artichokes are preferred for all my recipes, but frozen or canned hearts are very good. Store fresh artichokes in a plastic bag in the crisper drawer of a refrigerator for no more than five days.

Fettuccine with Veal and Artichoke Hearts

This is a family favorite in the autumn; there's something about a reduced wine sauce that everyone loves on a cool day. The recipe gets its inspiration from the cookery of Italy's northern provinces of the Veneto, Lombardy, and the Piedmont. The variation in the amount of butter I call for depends on how rich you want the final dish. The more the richer.

MAKES 4 SERVINGS

———

3 to 6 tablespoons unsalted butter
1 pound boneless veal shoulder, trimmed of fat and cut into
1/2-inch cubes
5 cooked artichoke hearts, preferably fresh (from 2 pounds
artichokes), chopped
1 cup dry white wine
Salt and freshly ground black pepper to taste
3/4 pound fettuccine
1 teaspoon finely chopped fresh parsley leaves
Freshly grated Parmesan cheese to taste

———

1. In a large skillet or casserole, melt 2 to 4 tablespoons of the butter over high heat. When the butter stops bubbling, add the veal and brown on all sides, about 4 minutes, stirring or shaking the pan. Add the artichoke hearts and continue cooking for 2 to 3 minutes. Add the wine and the remaining 1 or 2 tablespoons butter, season with salt

and pepper, and cook until the wine is nearly evaporated, about 5 minutes.

2. Meanwhile, bring a large pot of abundantly salted water to a rolling boil and ad the pasta. Drain when al dente and toss with the sauce in the skillet. Serve with a sprinkling of parsley and the cheese.

Wash the artichoke and cut off the top half of the bracts with a large, sharp knife. Remove the little bracts at the stem. Cut the stem off near the bottom so the artichoke can stand up. The stem flesh is edible, so slice off the outer layer and reserve. As you peel, slice, or break off the pale green bracts near the choke, discard them and then, with a paring knife, slice off the woody parts surrounding the bottom where the stem meets the foundation. In a circular motion, cut out the hairy choke. Once the artichoke is cut, it will blacken, so keep a lemon half nearby to immediately rub on the heart to prevent discoloration. As you finish each artichoke, put the heart in a bowl of water acidulated with lemon juice or vinegar and continue.

~

This famous cheese was originally made from water buffalo milk in the Campania region of Italy. Today, except for a small local production using water buffalo milk, it is made from cow's milk, with a huge portion of the worldwide production occurring in this country.

Mozzarella is a spun-curd cheese (page 10) and is best when eaten fresh. It is a soft, bland cheese with a milky flavor and dense texture. Fresh mozzarella should be dripping in its whey and springy to the touch. Domestic mozzarella is usually sold not fresh but as a hard, prepackaged product that lacks the distinctive taste of fresh. But feel free to use packaged mozzarella if your market doesn't carry fresh or if the cost of fresh mozzarella is excessive. When fresh mozzarella is made into small balls, it is called *bocconcini*,

Instant Lasagne

It's not really instant. This is the name of a thin, dried sheet of lasagne used for baking without having to preboil, as is traditional.

When I was growing up, one of the few Neapolitan dishes my mother would make was this lasagne, using the thicker lasagne sheets. It is a satisfying and rich dish that I often make on a Sunday and gladly eat all week, as will my children.

If your supermarket does not carry instant no-boil lasagne, you should tell the manager to get with the program. But remember; this recipe will not work with the regular lasagne noodles.

MAKES 4 SERVINGS PER BAKING PAN

————

2 pounds ricotta cheese, preferably fresh
2 large eggs
2 tablespoons sugar
4 large garlic cloves, finely chopped
1/2 teaspoon ground cinnamon
6 tablespoons extra-virgin olive oil
1 large red onion, chopped
1 1/4 pounds ground veal
Two 28-ounce cans crushed tomatoes
2 cups Chianti wine
2 tablespoons dried oregano
1 tablespoon dried thyme
1 bay leaf
Salt and freshly ground black pepper to taste

1 pound instant no-boil lasagne
2 pounds good-quality fresh mozzarella cheese, sliced

―――――

or *ovolini* if egg shaped. Mozzarella melts well and is the cheese most often used on pizzas.

1. In a large bowl, mix the ricotta cheese, eggs, sugar, garlic, and cinnamon.

2. In a large, deep stove-top casserole or a stockpot, heat the olive oil over high heat and cook the onion, stirring, until translucent, about 4 minutes. Add the veal and brown 2 to 3 minutes, then add the tomatoes, wine, and herbs and season with salt and pepper. Cook over high heat until the sauce is bubbling vigorously and is dense, reducing the heat to medium-low if the sauce is splattering too much, about 15 minutes. Turn the heat off, and let sit.

3. Arrange three 9-inch square aluminum baking pans side by side and lightly oil the bottom of each. Put a layer of lasagne down in each of the pans, then thinly spread a ladleful of the ricotta mixture over it. Cover with another sheet of lasagne, then a ladleful of tomato sauce. Now put down another sheet of lasagne and a layer of mozzarella (using up half of the mozzarella). Continue until all the ingredients are used up, finishing with a last layer of tomato sauce.

4. Preheat the oven to 350°F. Cover each pan with a sheet of aluminum foil and bake 45 minutes. They are done when the cheese is completely melted on top and the sauce around the perimeter is bubbling vigorously. Remove, let cool a bit to solidify, and serve or let cool completely and freeze. These will keep for up to 6 months. Reheat in a preheated 400°F oven by placing the aluminum foil-covered baking pans in the oven while still frozen and bake for about 1¼ hours.

Fresh mozzarella is imported from Italy, but there are many local producers, so you may want to check your supermarket and certainly a local Italian market.

Capellini with Ground Lamb
and Tomato Sauce

This is a delicious preparation for a cool fall day that everyone will enjoy. But remember that capellini is as thin as angel's hair and will be ruined if cooked too long. Read the directions on the package, and perhaps cook it even less than they recommend. Don't worry about the lard—it's used for flavoring, typical among Italian families living in mountain villages where it gives a rustic touch to the food, and you'll end up eating very little of it. If lard is simply out of the question, replace it with olive oil.

MAKES 4 SERVINGS

———

2 tablespoons lard
1 small onion, chopped
$^{1}/_{2}$ pound ground lamb (ask the butcher to grind it for you fresh)
$1^{1}/_{2}$ pounds ripe tomatoes, peeled, seeded, and finely chopped
2 tablespoons tomato paste
1 cup dry red wine
Freshly ground black pepper to taste
$^{3}/_{4}$ pound capellini
Freshly grated Pecorino cheese to taste

———

1. In a large skillet or casserole, melt the lard over high heat and cook the onion, stirring, until translucent, about 3 minutes. Add the ground lamb, breaking it up with a wooden spoon, and once it loses its pinkness, add the tomatoes, tomato paste, and wine. Reduce the heat to medium, stir well so the tomato paste is blended into the

sauce, and season with pepper. Cook until the sauce is thick, about 25 minutes, adding some water or more wine if it gets too thick.

2. Meanwhile, bring a large pot of abundantly salted water to a rolling boil and add the pasta. Drain when al dente. Turn the heat off under the sauce, add the capellini, and quickly toss well to coat. Serve with the cheese.

Penne with Lamb and Rosemary Sauce

Lamb and rosemary are a natural combination. In this simple recipe those robust flavors are excellent with the quill-shaped pasta called penne. I often make this when I don't want to put too much effort into dinner yet want something everyone will like.

MAKES 4 TO 6 SERVINGS

———

1 pound ground lamb (have the butcher grind it for you
fresh, if necessary)
3 tablespoons extra-virgin olive oil
2 shallots, finely chopped
3 garlic cloves, finely chopped
3 tablespoons very finely chopped fresh parsley leaves
One 28-ounce can crushed tomatoes
Leaves from 6 sprigs fresh rosemary, chopped
Salt and freshly ground black pepper to taste
1 pound penne
Freshly grated Pecorino cheese to taste

———

continued

1. Brown the ground lamb in a large skillet or casserole over medium heat, about 5 minutes, breaking up the meat with a wooden spoon. Remove with a slotted spoon, pressing out and discarding the fat. Set aside.

2. In the same skillet, heat the olive oil over medium-high heat and cook the shallots, garlic, and parsley until the shallots are soft, about 3 minutes, stirring frequently so the garlic doesn't burn. Add the lamb, tomatoes, and rosemary, season with salt and pepper, stir, reduce the heat to low, and simmer until thick, about 30 minutes.

3. Meanwhile, bring a large pot of abundantly salted water to a rolling boil and add the pasta. Drain when al dente and add to the sauce in the skillet. Toss until well coated and serve with the cheese.

Conchiglia with Pork and Peppers
in Shallot and Red Wine Sauce

*S*earing quickly locks in wonderful tastes. The sweet peppers, reds and yellows so inviting to the appetite, are a natural match for pork, and it's all covered with the aromatic and velvety flavor of the wine sauce.

MAKES 4 SERVINGS

———

¹/₂ cup extra-virgin olive oil

1 ounce salt pork, diced

4 shallots, chopped

3 garlic cloves, finely chopped

1 yellow bell pepper, seeded and sliced into strips

1 red bell pepper, seeded and sliced into strips

1 pound boneless pork spareribs, trimmed of fat and cut into cubes

1¹/₂ ounces soppresatta or salami (about 5 slices), sliced into strips

Salt and freshly ground black pepper to taste

1 tablespoon chopped fresh rosemary leaves

1 cup dry red wine

3 canned plum tomatoes

³/₄ pound conchiglia (shells)

Freshly grated Parmesan cheese to taste

———

1. In a large skillet or casserole, heat the olive oil over high heat and cook the salt pork for 1 minute or less. Add the shallots, garlic, and bell peppers and cook until softened, about 4 minutes, stirring

almost constantly so the garlic doesn't burn. Add the pork and sop-presatta, season with salt and pepper, and brown, stirring constantly, for 3 minutes. Sprinkle on the rosemary and stir well to mix. Pour in the wine and tomatoes, stirring to break up the tomatoes and cook until denser, about 4 minutes. Reduce the heat if the cooking is too lively.

2. Meanwhile, bring a large pot of abundantly salted water to a rolling boil and add the pasta. Drain when al dente. Add the pasta to the sauce in the skillet, toss together, and serve with the cheese.

Linguine Verde with Pork, Pancetta, and Cream Sauce

*O*ne rarely finds cream used in Italian cooking, and then only in some northern Italian regional cuisines, or in the *alta cucina* (haute cuisine) of famous restaurants. I tend to use cream only in the winter, and only when I want something indulgent and rib-stickingly good. This recipe has a great sauce and a subtle flavor, and was always a favorite with my kids when they were little. There is a temptation to keep adding things to a sauce, but you don't need too, just stick to the recipe.

MAKES 4 SERVINGS

_____

¹/₄ cup extra-virgin olive oil
¹/₄ pound pancetta, cut into thin strips
³/₄ pound boneless pork chops, cut into thin strips
2 garlic cloves, finely chopped
Salt and freshly ground black pepper to taste
¹/₂ cup dry white wine
¹/₂ cup heavy cream
³/₄ pound spinach linguine
Freshly grated Parmesan cheese to taste

———

1. In a large skillet or casserole, heat 3 tablespoons of the olive oil over medium-high heat and cook the pancetta, stirring, until slightly crisp, 2 to 3 minutes. Tilt the skillet and with a spoon remove and discard all the accumulated fat and olive oil. Add the pieces of pork, garlic, and the remaining tablespoon olive oil to the skillet and cook until the pork loses its color, 4 to 5 minutes, stirring constantly so the garlic doesn't burn. Season with salt and pepper. Pour in the wine and continue to cook until it is reduced by two-thirds. Pour in the cream and cook a few minutes more. Reduce the heat to very low to keep warm if the pasta is still cooking.

2. Meanwhile, bring a large pot of abundantly salted water to a rolling boil and add the pasta. Drain when al dente and toss with the sauce in the skillet. Serve with abundant cheese.

Linguine Verde with Panfried Pork and Red Bell Peppers

*O*h, this is good! It's very simple and quick, which as you now know means you've got to pay attention. Searing the pork gives it a crispy outside and a juicy inside, while the sauce is simply made from any high-quality jarred or Italian deli-bought roasted red bell pepper seasoned with lots of garlic and rosemary.

MAKES 2 LARGE SERVINGS

1/4 cup extra-virgin olive oil
3 garlic cloves, 1 crushed and 2 very finely chopped
Two 3/4-inch-thick pork chops, about 10 ounces each
Salt and freshly ground white pepper to taste
Leaves from 1 sprig fresh rosemary, chopped
2 roasted red bell peppers, peeled or 2 jarred peppers, chopped with their oil or juice
1/2 pound spinach linguine

---

1. In a blue steel or other highly heat-conductive skillet, heat 2 tablespoons of the olive oil over medium heat and cook the crushed garlic for about 30 seconds. Remove and discard the garlic. Raise the heat to medium-high. Place the pork chops in the pan, season with salt and pepper, and cook until golden brown on both sides and cooked through, about 10 minutes altogether, turning once.

2. In another skillet, heat the remaining 2 tablespoons olive oil over medium heat and cook the chopped garlic, rosemary, and roasted

pepper until the mixture is soft and fragrant, about 10 minutes, stirring frequently so the garlic doesn't burn and lowering the heat if it is cooking too fast.

3. Meanwhile, bring a large pot of abundantly salted water to a rolling boil and add the pasta. Drain when al dente and toss in the skillet with the red pepper and garlic. Transfer to a serving bowl or platter and place the pork chops on top. Serve immediately.

NOTE: You can also grill the chops. Coat with oil and rosemary and grill for about 10 minutes a side.

The quintessential Italian herb, oregano is excellent both fresh and dried. This perennial plant is ideal for an herb garden or pot. To get the oregano flower buds needed for this recipe, you will need to grow your own plant. Do not wash fresh oregano until needed.

~

Linguine with Grilled Pork Chops and Oregano Flower Buds

Fantastic with dried oregano and simply heaven with the oregano flower buds. The buds are picked with the leaves just before the plant flowers. They're chopped up and tossed with the pasta while the pork chops are grilling.

MAKES 4 SERVINGS

————

4 boneless center-cut pork chops (about 1 1/2 pounds),
trimmed of fat
Salt and freshly ground black pepper to taste
6 tablespoons extra-virgin olive oil
1 tablespoon dried oregano
3/4 pound linguine
Leaves and buds from 10 sprigs fresh oregano, chopped, or 1/4 cup
finely chopped fresh oregano leaves
1/2 cup freshly grated Parmesan cheese

————

1. Prepare a hot charcoal fire or preheat a gas grill on high for 20 minutes. Between 2 pieces of waxed paper, pound the pork chops until about 2/3 inch thick with a mallet or the side of a heavy cleaver. Place the pork chops in a glass or ceramic baking pan, season with salt and pepper, drizzle with 2 tablespoons of the olive oil, and sprinkle with the dried oregano on both sides. Place on the grill and cook 5 minutes a side, turning once and basting with the olive oil accumulated in the pan.

2. Meanwhile, bring a large pot of abundantly salted water to a rolling boil and add the pasta. Drain when al dente and toss with the remaining 1/4 cup olive oil, more black pepper, the oregano leaves and buds, and the cheese. Transfer to a serving platter. Arrange the pork chops on top of the linguine and serve.

Malfadine with Chicken and Ricotta Almond Sauce

Malfadine is an irregularly cut pasta, usually a width wider than fettuccine with one ragged edge. I find this dish ideal as a spring dinner. Chop the onion, garlic, and parsley together for a quick soffritto to get the sauce going.

MAKES 4 SERVINGS

———

1/4 cup extra-virgin olive oil
3 tablespoons very finely chopped onion
2 garlic cloves, very finely chopped
1/4 cup very finely chopped fresh parsley leaves
1/2 pound boneless chicken breast, skin removed and cut into small cubes
1/2 cup dry white wine
3/4 pound malfadine
1/2 pound ricotta cheese, preferably fresh
1/4 cup finely ground roasted almonds
1/2 cup freshly grated Parmesan cheese
Freshly ground black pepper to taste
Cayenne pepper (optional) to taste

———

continued

1. In a large skillet or casserole, heat the olive oil and cook the onion, garlic, and parsley over medium-high heat until the onion turns translucent, about 4 minutes, stirring frequently. Add the chicken pieces, stirring, and after 1 minute add the wine. Cook until there is no pink left to any of the chicken pieces, 3 to 4 minutes, then remove the chicken with a slotted spoon and set aside. Reduce the wine to a syrupy sauce.

2. Meanwhile, bring a large pot of abundantly salted water to a rolling boil and add the pasta. Drain when al dente. Beat the ricotta and almonds together until well blended. Return the chicken to the skillet, then add the pasta, ricotta-almond mixture, and Parmesan and toss well with black pepper to taste. Sprinkle with cayenne pepper, if using, and serve immediately.

Linguine with Peppery Chicken and Tomato Sauce

Although this recipe sounds simply hot, it's a powerfully aromatic dish that is quite satisfying. The recipe utilizes leftover chicken in a tomato sauce seasoned with garlic and oregano. Younger kids will probably find the pepper too hot.

MAKES 4 SERVINGS

———

3 tablespoons extra-virgin olive oil
1/4 cup finely chopped onion
1 garlic clove, chopped
1 fresh green chili pepper, seeded and finely chopped
1 pound ripe tomatoes, peeled, seeded, and finely chopped
1/2 cup dry white wine
Salt and freshly ground black pepper to taste
1 cup finely chopped cooked chicken meat
2 tablespoons finely chopped fresh oregano leaves
3/4 pound linguine

———

1. In a large skillet or casserole, heat the olive oil over medium heat and cook the onion, garlic, and chili pepper until soft, 5 to 6 minutes, stirring frequently. Add the tomatoes and wine, season with salt and pepper, and cook until dense, about 20 minutes. Add the chicken and oregano and cook for 5 minutes, stirring occasionally.

2. Meanwhile, bring a large pot of abundantly salted water to a rolling boil and add the pasta. Drain when al dente and toss with the sauce in the skillet. Serve immediately.

Lasagne with Chicken, Spinach, and Portobello Mushrooms

Lasagne does not always have to follow the familiar recipe of ragù, mozzarella, and ricotta cheese. In this recipe, the flavors are enhanced with fresh basil, the earthy taste of portobello mushrooms, and the appealing green of spinach. This recipe is most conveniently made in three 9-inch square aluminum baking pans.

MAKES 4 SERVINGS PER BAKING PAN

———

1/2 cup extra-virgin olive oil

1 medium-size onion, finely chopped

3 garlic cloves, finely chopped

Two 28-ounce cans crushed tomatoes

Salt and freshly ground black pepper to taste

10 large fresh basil leaves

1 1/4 pounds boneless chicken breast halves, skin removed and pounded into thin scallopine between 2 pieces of waxed paper with a mallet or side of a heavy cleaver

1/2 pound portobello mushroom caps, sliced

10 ounces fresh spinach, trimmed of tough stems and thoroughly washed

1 pound instant no-boil lasagne noodles

1 pound ricotta cheese, preferably fresh

1 pound fresh or commercially packaged Fiore di Latte or mozzarella cheese, thinly sliced

———

1. Heat ¼ cup of the olive oil in a large skillet or casserole over medium-high heat and cook the onion and garlic until the onion is translucent, 7 to 8 minutes, stirring frequently so the garlic doesn't burn. Add the tomatoes, season with salt and pepper, and cook over medium-high heat until denser, about 20 minutes, stirring so the bottom doesn't blacken. Turn the heat off and add the basil to steep until the sauce is needed.

2. Heat the remaining ¼ cup olive oil in a large nonstick skillet over medium-high heat and cook the chicken until light golden brown, 3 to 4 minutes per side. Remove the chicken to a plate and set aside.

3. In the same skillet, cook the mushroom caps until dark golden brown on both sides, about 4 minutes altogether. Remove from the pan and set aside.

4. In the same skillet, wilt the spinach in handfuls, adding 1 to 2 tablespoons water as you do, until all the spinach is wilted, 3 to 4 minutes in all. Drain and set aside.

5. Spoon a few tablespoons of the tomato sauce in the bottom of each of three 9-inch square aluminum baking pans. Layer the ingredients in each pan in this order: lasagne, sauce, spinach, salt, pepper, mushrooms, lasagne, ricotta, sauce, lasagne, chicken, salt, pepper, sauce, lasagne, mozzarella, and sauce.

6. Preheat the oven to 400°F. Cover each pan with a tented sheet of aluminum foil and bake until the cheese on top is completely melted and the sauce on the sides of the pan is bubbling vigorously, about 35 minutes. Let cool a few minutes to solidify and serve or cool completely and freeze. It will keep up to 3 months.

NOTE: To reheat, preheat the oven to 400°F and place the frozen lasagne in the oven for 1¼ hours.

CHAPTER SIX

Pasta with Seafood

THE MOST POPULAR seafood condiment for macaroni in Italy is the humble salted anchovy. You will find it used in many preparations with, and without, seafood. As with meat and pasta, seafood is used as a condiment with pasta and the portions are kept smaller than they are when the seafood is served alone. It goes without saying that the fresher your seafood, the better will be the final preparation. The three essential pantry products that make pasta with seafood so easy for the family cook are the previously mentioned salted anchovy, canned sardines in oil, and canned tuna. These are great flavor enhancers and don't need much more than a heating when prepared with other ingredients or sauces.

Linguine with Anchovy and Parsley Butter

This is a quick "midnight" pasta or *spaghettata*, a category of pasta preparations made late in the evening when one comes home from the movies or the theater with a little bit of an appetite. If you don't have the time to make the butter, chop everything anyway and toss with the steaming pasta.

MAKES 4 SERVINGS

———

¾ pound linguine
6 tablespoons Anchovy and Parsley Butter (page 3)

———

1. Bring a large pot of abundantly salted water to a rolling boil, and add the pasta.

2. Drain when al dente and toss well with the anchovy butter in a large serving bowl.

Spaghetti with Oregano, Garlic, and Anchovy Sauce

This spaghetti preparation is usually served with or before fish, without cheese. It is based on a *salsa crudo*, or raw sauce, an uncooked sauce that you toss with steaming hot pasta. The garlic, anchovy, and oregano certainly provide enough flavor for this dish to stand on its own, but it's even better with a little piece of grilled fish.

MAKES 4 SERVINGS

———

1 pound spaghetti
1/2 cup extra-virgin olive oil
4 garlic cloves, finely chopped
2 tablespoons dried oregano
8 salted anchovy fillets, rinsed, patted dry, and chopped

———

1. Bring a large pot of abundantly salted water to a rolling boil and add the pasta. Drain when al dente.

2. While the pasta is cooking, stir the olive oil, garlic, oregano, and anchovies together in a large serving bowl. Toss with the hot pasta and serve immediately.

Spaghetti with Anchovies, Herbs, and Spices

Keeping it simple does not mean keeping it dull. Take this preparation with its terrific, and classic, taste. All you've done is cook the spaghetti—the rest is part of a raw sauce, a *salsa crudo*. And it goes great with Skillet-Fried Steak with Black, White, and Red Peppers (page 183).

MAKES 4 TO 6 SERVINGS

———

1¹/₄ pounds spaghetti
¹/₄ to ¹/₂ cup extra-virgin olive oil
4 garlic cloves, finely chopped
10 salted anchovy fillets, rinsed, patted dry, and chopped
1 tablespoon dried oregano
¹/₄ cup finely chopped fresh parsley leaves
2 dried red chili peppers, crumbled, or ¹/₂ teaspoon
red pepper flakes
Freshly ground black pepper to taste

———

1. Bring a large pot of abundantly salted water to a rolling boil and add the pasta. Drain when al dente.

2. While the pasta is cooking, mix the remaining ingredients in a large serving bowl. Toss the pasta with the sauce to evenly coat and serve.

Penne with Tomato and Anchovy Sauce

A family favorite that can be eaten hot or at room temperature. You might think that the amount of anchovies is excessive, but they are not—trust me. You're going to get a powerfully good taste. The leftovers can be used for Baked Penne with Tomato and Anchovy Sauce (page 130).

MAKES 4 SERVINGS

———

¹/₄ cup extra-virgin olive oil
2 garlic cloves, crushed
2 cups canned crushed tomatoes
10 salted anchovy fillets, rinsed and patted dry
Salt and freshly ground black pepper to taste
³/₄ pound penne

———

1. In a large skillet or casserole, heat the olive oil over high heat and cook the garlic until it begins to turn light brown, about 1 minute or less. Remove the garlic and discard. Add the tomatoes and anchovies, and season with salt and pepper. Cook until the sauce is thick, about 10 minutes, or 30 minutes on a medium heat.

2. Meanwhile, bring a large pot of abundantly salted water to a rolling boil and add the pasta. Drain when al dente. Toss the pasta with the sauce in the skillet and serve.

Baked Penne with Tomato and Anchovy Sauce

Leftovers sometimes get a bad reputation, but artfully combined they can result in magnificent tastes. This recipe is a quick mix of two other recipes. It's fast and delicious.

MAKES 2 SERVINGS

———

4 cups Penne with Tomato and Anchovy Sauce (page 129)
2 cups Green and Yellow Salad (page 22)
2 tablespoons extra-virgin olive oil
Pinch of cayenne pepper (optional)
$1/2$ pound mozzarella cheese, sliced

———

1. Preheat the oven to 400°F.

2. Toss together the penne, salad, olive oil, and cayenne pepper, if desired. Arrange in a medium-size baking pan and cover with the mozzarella. Bake until the cheese melts, 10 to 15 minutes, and serve.

Perciatelli with Egg and Anchovy Sauce

Here's another "midnight" pasta that is quite satisfying when you're hungry and don't want to put much effort into preparation and cooking.

MAKES 2 SERVINGS

———

3 tablespoons extra-virgin olive oil
1 large garlic clove, finely chopped
6 salted anchovy fillets, rinsed and patted dry
½ pound perciatelli
1 medium-size egg, hard-boiled, shelled, and finely chopped
1 teaspoon finely chopped fresh parsley leaves
Freshly ground black pepper to taste
Freshly grated Parmesan cheese to taste

———

1. Put the olive oil, garlic, and anchovies in a small skillet. Warm over low heat until the anchovies melt into the olive oil. Turn the heat off.

2. Meanwhile, bring a large pot of abundantly salted water to a rolling boil and add the perciatelli. Drain when al dente and transfer to a large serving bowl. Toss with the melted anchovy mixture. Sprinkle over the chopped egg and parsley and toss again. Serve with black pepper and Parmesan cheese to pass around.

Penne Rigate with Melted Sardine and Red Sauce

Ridged quill-shaped pasta called penne rigate are tossed with a thick sauce—what the Italians call *sugo*—that is typical in Sicily. The sauce begins with a delicate soffritto and then the other ingredients are melted in until it becomes a rich sauce with an aromatic bouquet.

MAKES 4 SERVINGS

––––––

1/4 cup extra-virgin olive oil
1 small onion, finely chopped
2 garlic cloves, finely chopped
2 tablespoons finely chopped fresh parsley leaves
One 4-ounce can sardines packed in olive oil
4 salted anchovy fillets, rinsed and patted dry
1 teaspoon capers, rinsed
*1 large fresh artichoke heart, boiled in water to cover until tender,
drained, and chopped, or 2 small canned artichoke hearts*
1 1/4 cups tomato puree, preferably fresh
2 tablespoons water
1 teaspoon dried oregano
Pinch of cayenne pepper
Salt and freshly ground black pepper to taste
1 pound penne rigate
Freshly grated Pecorino Pepato or Pecorino cheese to taste

––––––

1. In a large skillet or casserole, heat the olive oil over medium-high heat and cook the onion, garlic, and parsley until the onion is soft,

3 to 4 minutes, shaking or stirring frequently so the garlic doesn't burn. Add the sardines, anchovies, capers, and artichoke heart and cook for 2 minutes, stirring. Add the tomato puree, water, oregano, and cayenne pepper, season with salt and black pepper, reduce the heat to medium, and cook until dense, about 12 minutes.

2. Meanwhile, bring a large pot of abundantly salted water to a rolling boil and add the pasta. Drain when al dente and toss with the sauce in the skillet. Remove to a serving platter and serve with cheese.

Linguine with Sardines, Olives, and Green Peppers

The sauce for this recipe begins with a soffritto of onion, garlic, celery, peperoncini, and chili pepper. Melted into it are sardines, anchovies, tomatoes, olives, and capers. The result is a robust taste, a perfect complement for linguine.

MAKES 4 SERVINGS

---

4 to 6 tablespoons extra-virgin olive oil

1 small onion, chopped

2 garlic cloves, finely chopped

1/2 celery stalk, finely chopped

1 peperoncini (Italian long pepper), seeded and chopped

1 fresh green chili pepper, seeded and chopped

One 4-ounce can sardines packed in water, drained

4 salted anchovy fillets, rinsed and patted dry

1 1/2 cups canned plum tomatoes with their juices

6 large imported green olives, pitted and chopped

1 tablespoon capers, rinsed and chopped

2 tablespoons chopped fresh parsley leaves

Salt and freshly ground black pepper to taste

3/4 pound linguine

---

1. In a large skillet or casserole, heat the olive oil over medium-high heat and cook the onion, garlic, celery, and peppers until soft, about 8 minutes, stirring frequently. Add the sardines and anchovies and

cook until they melt, about 1 minute. Add the tomatoes and cook until denser, about 8 minutes, stirring. Add the olives, capers, and parsley, season with salt and pepper, and cook for 1 to 2 minutes. Turn the heat off and let the sauce sit in the pan while you finish cooking the pasta.

2. Meanwhile, bring a large pot of abundantly salted water to a rolling boil and add the pasta. Drain when al dente and toss well with the sauce in the skillet.

Orecchiette with Beet Leaves, Tuna, and Olives

Orecchiette, or "little ears," are a favorite pasta shape in the southern Italian region of Apulia, the heel of the Italian boot. They are made by rolling a long, thick rope of semolina pasta dough, cutting small sections off, and pressing down with one's thumb before setting them out to dry.

In this recipe beet leaves are wilted in a pan, then tossed with olives and tuna *sott'olio,* or tuna preserved in olive oil. Beet leaves can be a touch bitter, so I think you will find the balance of tuna, garlic, and olives enhanced by the abundant use of Pecorino cheese and red pepper flakes.

MAKES 2 SERVINGS

continued

¹/₄ cup extra-virgin olive oil

3 cups thoroughly washed loosely packed chopped beet leaves (stems discarded)

Salt and freshly ground black pepper to taste

2 salted anchovy fillets, rinsed, patted dry, and chopped

2 garlic cloves, finely chopped

1 tablespoon finely chopped fresh parsley leaves

15 imported black olives, pitted and chopped

One 4-ounce can imported tuna packed in olive oil

¹/₂ pound orecchiette

Freshly grated Pecorino or Parmesan cheese to taste

Red chili pepper flakes to taste

---

1. In large skillet or casserole, heat the olive oil over medium-high heat with the beet leaves, season with salt and pepper, and cook until the leaves wilt, about 3 minutes. Add the anchovies, garlic, parsley, and olives and cook for 3 minutes. Turn the heat off and toss with the tuna.

2. Meanwhile, bring a large pot of abundantly salted water to a rolling boil and add the pasta. Drain when al dente and toss with the sauce in the skillet. Sprinkle with cheese and red pepper flakes and toss again. Serve immediately.

Linguine with Anchovy, Caper, and Mint Sauce

A warm bath of olive oil for the pungent concoction of anchovies, capers, lemon, mint, and tomato makes this Sicilian-inspired sauce a delight tossed with pasta.

MAKES 4 SERVINGS

---

10 salted anchovy fillets, rinsed, patted dry, and chopped
2 tablespoons capers, rinsed and chopped if large
1/4 cup finely chopped fresh mint leaves
3 large garlic cloves, finely chopped
2 teaspoons grated lemon zest
4 ripe plum tomatoes (10 to 12 ounces), peeled, seeded, drained well, and chopped
1/4 to 1/2 cup extra-virgin olive oil
Salt and freshly ground black pepper to taste
3/4 pound linguine
Chopped fresh parsley or mint leaves for garnish

---

1. Mix the anchovies, capers, mint, garlic, lemon zest, and tomatoes. Pour the olive oil in a large skillet or casserole and stir the tomato mixture in gently. Turn the heat to medium and cook for 5 minutes, stirring occasionally. If it starts to bubble fast, turn the heat off. Season with salt and pepper.

2. Meanwhile, bring a large pot of abundantly salted water to a rolling boil and add the linguine. Drain when al dente. Toss with the linguine, sprinkle with parsley, and serve immediately or let it stand for 5 minutes to let the flavors mingle.

The caper is a bushy perennial plant indigenous to the Mediterranean that grows out of old stone walls and cliffs. The best capers are found sold by weight and stored in salt or brine at Italian markets. They usually are large, and must be rinsed before using in the recipe. Supermarkets sell jarred capers of different brands, most often called "nonpareil," which are unnecessarily more expensive.

Linguine with Tuna and Green Beans

When I must cook for both adults and children, I face a dilemma. The adults don't want boring "kid food" and children are finicky, all to a different degree. I refuse to slave over two separate meals, so I rely on this quick preparation that seems to fit the gustatory bill, pleasing all kinds of palates.

MAKES 4 TO 6 SERVINGS

¹/₄ cup extra-virgin olive oil
1 garlic clove, finely chopped
Three 4-ounce cans tuna packed in water, drained
¹/₂ cup loosely packed fresh oregano leaves, finely chopped
Salt and freshly ground black pepper to taste
1 pound linguine
¹/₂ pound green beans, trimmed and cut into ¹/₂-inch lengths

1. In a large skillet or casserole, heat the olive oil over medium-high heat with the garlic, tuna, and oregano. Once it begins to sizzle, cook for 2 minutes, then remove from the heat. Season with salt and pepper.

2. Meanwhile, bring a large pot of abundantly salted water to a rolling boil and add the pasta. After 5 minutes add the green beans and continue cooking. Drain when the pasta is al dente. Pour the pasta and green beans in with the tuna and toss until well coated. Serve immediately.

Fusilli with Red Tuna Sauce

Here's another fast way to use a can of tuna with pasta. The corkscrew-shaped pasta called fusilli is perfect for this sauce from western Sicily, made with pine nuts and raisins. Reserve ¼ cup of the sauce and you can make Chick-peas and Artichoke Hearts with Red Tuna Sauce (page 255).

————

¼ *cup extra-virgin olive oil*
¼ *cup finely chopped onion*
2 garlic cloves, 1 crushed and 1 finely chopped
3 cups canned crushed tomatoes
Salt and freshly ground black pepper to taste
1 tablespoon pine nuts
1 tablespoon raisins
2 tablespoons finely chopped fresh parsley leaves
1 pound fusilli
One 6½-ounce can imported tuna packed in oil

————

1. In a large skillet or casserole, heat the olive oil over medium-high heat and cook the onion and crushed garlic until softened, about 3 minutes, stirring frequently so the garlic doesn't burn. Add the tomatoes and cook until denser, about 12 minutes, stirring occasionally. Remove from the heat, season with salt and pepper, and stir in the pine nuts, raisins, and parsley.

continued

2. Meanwhile, bring a large pot of abundantly salted water to a rolling boil and add the pasta. Drain when al dente.

3. Add the tuna with its oil to the tomato sauce. Toss the fusilli with the sauce in the skillet and serve.

Bavette with Tuna

*W*hen my children were little, they would actually ask me to make this favorite dish. I first had it myself while waiting for a train in Milan. It is so subtle and satisfying. *Bavette* is another name for fettuccine.

MAKES 4 SERVINGS

———

1 pound fettuccine
4 to 6 tablespoons (3/4 stick) unsalted butter
Leaves from 12 sprigs fresh parsley, finely chopped
Three 4-ounce cans tuna packed in water, drained

———

1. Bring a large pot of abundantly salted water to a rolling boil and add the pasta. Drain when al dente.

2. While the pasta cooks, melt the butter with the parsley in a large skillet or casserole over medium-high heat. Remove from the heat once the butter is melted and begins to bubble. Stir in the tuna. Toss with the fettuccine in the skillet and serve immediately.

Bavette con Salsa Rossa di Tonno alla Diavolo

I fancy this seductive Italian name over the English because it sounds more enticing. Basically, it is a spicy hot (*diavolo*) red (*rossa*) sauce (*salsa*) made with tomatoes and tuna (*tonno*) for a kind of fettuccine (*bavette*). The flavors meld together slowly when off the heat. It's delicious and very easy to make.

MAKES 4 SERVINGS

———

3 tablespoons extra-virgin olive oil
1½ cups canned or fresh chopped ripe plum tomatoes
Two 4-ounce cans tuna packed in olive oil
4 to 6 tablespoons (¾ stick) unsalted butter
¼ cup finely chopped fresh parsley leaves
3 garlic cloves, finely chopped
Cayenne pepper to taste
Salt and freshly ground black pepper to taste
1 pound fettuccine

———

1. In a large skillet or casserole, heat the olive oil over medium-high heat. Add the tomatoes and cook, stirring, until some juice evaporates, about 3 minutes. Turn the heat off, add everything but the fettuccine, and mix well.

2. Meanwhile, bring a large pot of abundantly salted water to a rolling boil and add the pasta. Drain when al dente. Toss with the sauce in the skillet and serve immediately.

Spaghetti with Red Tuna Sauce, Spinach, and Swiss Chard

I like the colorful contrast of red and green in this appealing spaghetti dish with a mild tuna flavor, and I find that children really like it.

MAKES 4 TO 6 SERVINGS

———

2 cups tomato puree, preferably fresh
1/2 cup extra-virgin olive oil
One 4-ounce can tuna packed in olive oil
2 salted anchovy fillets, rinsed and patted dry
1 teaspoon dried oregano
Salt and freshly ground black pepper to taste
2 tablespoons unsalted butter
6 tablespoons finely chopped onion
3 garlic cloves, finely chopped
6 to 8 ounces fresh spinach, trimmed of tough stems, thoroughly washed, and chopped
6 to 8 ounces Swiss chard leaves, trimmed of tough stems and ribs, thoroughly washed, and chopped
Juice from 1/2 lemon
1 pound spaghetti

———

1. In a large skillet or casserole, heat the tomato puree over low heat with 6 tablespoons of the olive oil, the tuna with its oil, the anchovies, and oregano and season with salt and pepper.

2. Meanwhile, heat the remaining 2 tablespoons olive oil with the butter in a large skillet over medium heat. Once the butter has melted and stopped bubbling, cook the onion and garlic until translucent, about 6 minutes, stirring frequently so the garlic doesn't burn. Add the spinach, Swiss chard, and lemon juice and cook until the leaves wilt.

3. Meanwhile, bring a large pot of abundantly salted water to a rolling boil and add the pasta. Drain when al dente. Toss with the tomato sauce in the skillet, then add the spinach and Swiss chard and toss again. Serve immediately.

Fettuccine with Swordfish Gnocchi
and Light Tomato Sauce

Italian dumplings are called gnocchi, and although that usually means they are made of semolina or potatoes, this recipe twists the concept a bit and uses swordfish. In fact, they are similar to the French quenelles. The secret is to make them light but not so light that they fall apart in the broth.

MAKES 4 TO 6 SERVINGS

---

2 large egg yolks

3 tablespoons pine nuts

1½ pounds swordfish steaks, skin removed

1 teaspoon dried oregano

½ teaspoon freshly ground white pepper

Salt and freshly ground black pepper to taste

2 tablespoons extra-virgin olive oil

2 tablespoons unsalted butter

1 small onion, finely chopped

2 garlic cloves, finely chopped

1 cup dry white wine

2½ cups crushed fresh tomatoes or one 1¾-pound can crushed tomatoes

1 pound fettuccine

---

1. Beat the egg yolks in a medium-size bowl. Finely grind the pine nuts in a food processor. Remove and add to the egg yolks. Grind the

swordfish in the food processor to a paste. Add to the mixing bowl. Sprinkle the mixture with ½ teaspoon of the oregano and the white pepper and season with salt and black pepper.

2. In a large skillet or casserole, heat the olive oil and butter together over medium-high heat. Once the butter has melted and the bubbling subsided, cook the onion and garlic until soft, 3 to 4 minutes, stirring frequently so the garlic doesn't burn. Pour in the wine, the remaining ½ teaspoon oregano, and the tomatoes and season with salt and black pepper. Just as the sauce begins to bubble, form the swordfish mixture into dumplings using 2 tablespoons or soup spoons (not your hands) to make oval-shaped pieces. Drop them into the sauce. Once all the dumplings are in the sauce, shake the pan, cover it with the lid, reduce the heat to medium, and cook until each is springy to the touch, about 12 minutes.

3. Meanwhile, bring a large pot of abundantly salted water to a rolling boil and add the pasta. Drain when al dente and transfer to a serving platter or bowl, spoon the sauce over, arrange the gnocchi on top or around the edges, and serve.

Many families don't fry foods at home because they are rightly worried about dietary fat. But frying does not have to mean increased fat consumption. Properly fried food uses less oil than is used in most salad dressings. Italians fry at home and they usually use olive oil, the cooking oil with the highest amount of monounsaturated fat.

To avoid greasy fried foods you need to understand the principles of frying. First, use clean oil that is kept consistently hot throughout the cooking. Second, never crowd the pan with too much food, or the temperature of the oil will drop too low and the food will absorb the oil and become greasy instead of crispy. The temperature of the oil must be kept between 350 and 375°F. If you have neither a deep fryer with regulated heat controls nor a candy thermometer to

Linguine with Swordfish Nuggets

You can never go wrong with golden-crusted fritters. When my children were young, fried foods had to be called "nuggets." This recipe will give you a taste of swordfish I believe you've never had before, not to mention a reason to come up with a description better than "nugget."

MAKES 4 SERVINGS

———

1½ pounds swordfish steaks, cut into bite-size rectangles
1 large egg, lightly beaten
1 cup dry bread crumbs mixed with ½ cup all-purpose flour and 1 teaspoon salt
1 cup plus 3 tablespoons extra-virgin olive oil
2 garlic cloves, finely chopped
1 teaspoon finely chopped lemon zest
3 tablespoons finely chopped fresh parsley leaves
3 tablespoons finely chopped fresh mint leaves
4 salted anchovy fillets, rinsed and patted dry
Salt and freshly ground black pepper to taste
1 pound linguine

———

1. Dip the swordfish pieces in the beaten egg and dredge in the bread crumb mixture, tapping off any excess. Set aside on a tray in the refrigerator until needed.

2. In a large skillet or casserole, heat 1 cup of the olive oil over medium-high heat until it is nearly smoking, about 10 minutes. In a

small skillet, heat the remaining 3 tablespoons olive oil over medium-high heat.

3. Add the garlic, lemon zest, parsley, mint, and anchovies to the small skillet, stirring for 1 minute. Turn the heat off.

4. Fry the fish pieces without crowding them until golden brown in the large skillet, about 2 minutes a side, turning with long tongs. Remove the swordfish pieces with a slotted spoon, set on paper towels to drain, season with salt and pepper, and keep warm.

5. Meanwhile, bring a large pot of abundantly salted water to a rolling boil and add the pasta. Drain when al dente and toss in the skillet with the garlic, lemon zest, and herb mixture along with 3 tablespoons of the oil that the fish was fried in. Transfer to a serving platter, arrange the fish on top, and serve.

measure temperature, then a good rule of thumb is that it takes a saucepan 8 inches in diameter at the top and 6 inches on the bottom filled with 6 cups of oil to a depth of about 2¼ inches about 10 minutes over high heat to achieve the right temperature before you commence deep-frying.

Deep-fried food must always drain before serving to allow excess oil to drip off. Transfer the fried foods to a paper towel-lined tray or platter while you continue cooking. The cooled deep-frying oil can be saved by straining it through paper oil strainers sold at kitchen supply stores and through the manufacturers of home-use deep fryers. It is best to discard the oil after the fourth or fifth use.

Trenette with Smooth Smoked Salmon and Shrimp Sauce

This is an amazing preparation, rich, creamy, and utterly delicious. Trenette is a kind of pasta in northern Italy that can be replaced with fettuccine.

MAKES 4 TO 6 SERVINGS

———

1/4 pound shrimp, shelled (save the shells)
1 cup water
1 tablespoon shelled raw pistachios
1/4 pound smoked Irish, Scottish, or Norwegian salmon
2 tablespoons finely chopped onion
1 garlic clove, peeled
1 tablespoon finely chopped fresh parsley leaves
1/2 teaspoon salt
1/2 teaspoon freshly ground white pepper
1/4 teaspoon cayenne pepper
2 tablespoons Marsala wine
1 tablespoon freshly squeezed lemon juice
1 cup heavy cream
3 tablespoons unsalted butter
Freshly ground black pepper to taste
1 pound trenette
Finely chopped fresh parsley leaves for garnish

———

1. Put the shrimp shells in a pot with the water and bring to a boil, then reduce to very low and simmer until needed in step 3.

2. Place the pistachios in a food processor and grind. Add the shrimp, salmon, onion, garlic, parsley, salt, and white and cayenne peppers and process in short bursts until chopped. Stir the Marsala, lemon juice, and cream together in a small bowl. Set the processor on puree and run continuously while you slowly pour in the cream mixture through the feed tube. You will have about 2 cups of thick puree.

3. In a medium-size skillet, melt the butter, then pour in the puree and cook over medium-high heat for 2 minutes, stirring. Strain the shrimp broth (you should have about ½ cup). Reduce the heat under the puree to low and simmer, stirring in ¼ cup of the shrimp broth until thick, creamy, and somewhat smooth. Taste and correct the salt, pepper, or cayenne.

4. Meanwhile, bring a large pot of abundantly salted water to a rolling boil and add the pasta. Drain when al dente. Toss the pasta with the sauce in the skillet until evenly coated. Serve immediately with freshly ground black pepper and a sprinkling of parsley.

Spaghetti with Bluefish

My first experience with bluefish was when I lived on Long Island. In New England, where I later lived, bluefish is also a very popular fish. When the blues run it is a magnificent sight, and dangerous if you are in the water, because these voracious fish swim in schools, churning the water like an eggbeater, their sharp teeth slicing through anything in the way. They're pretty easy to catch, but deteriorate rapidly after being caught because of their high oil content, their taste changing from delicious to bland in a day. I've seen this myself when I made this recipe for friends once: the bluefish was so fresh, about three hours old, that no one recognized what the fish was, only having had the older and duller store-bought bluefish. Moral of the story: it's more important to use fresh fish than bluefish in this recipe.

MAKES 2 TO 3 SERVINGS

———

3/4 pound bluefish or other oily firm-fleshed fish fillets, skin
removed and cut into small pieces
All-purpose flour for dredging
Salt
3 tablespoons extra-virgin olive oil
1 small onion, peeled and finely chopped
1 1/4 cups dry white wine
1 1/2 cups canned tomato puree
1 fresh red chili pepper, stem removed
Freshly ground black pepper to taste
1/4 cup finely chopped fresh parsley leaves
1/2 pound spaghetti

———

1. Dredge the fish pieces in the flour, salt lightly, and tap off any excess flour. Set aside.

2. Heat the olive oil in a skillet or casserole, preferably earthenware, over high heat and cook the onion until translucent, 2 to 3 minutes, stirring. Add the floured pieces of fish and cook until golden, about 2 minutes per side, and remove with a slotted spoon. Set aside.

3. Pour 1 cup of the wine into the casserole and deglaze over high heat, scraping up any browned bits off the bottom. When half of the wine has evaporated, add the tomato puree and chili pepper and season with salt and pepper. Stir, reduce the heat to medium-low, and simmer until syrupy, about 20 minutes. Return the fish to the casserole, turn the heat to medium, and cook until the fish is about to flake, about 8 minutes. Add the parsley and a few tablespoons more wine if necessary to thin the sauce. Stir well.

4. Meanwhile, bring a large pot of abundantly salted water to a rolling boil and add the pasta. Drain when al dente and add to the sauce in the casserole. Toss well and serve.

Every family loves crusty country-style Italian or French bread to accompany their meals—anyway, I know mine does. Good-quality French and Italian breads are now being made across the country, crusty golden even if they're not close to the real thing. In Italy of the Middle Ages, bread was the foundation of the family meal and everything else was called an "accompaniment to bread."

Rather than keep bread in a bread box, which one can certainly do, I like to freeze unused portions. Bread defrosts quickly, too. When I call for bread crumbs, I mean dry bread crumbs made from leftover Italian or French bread. Leave the bread on a tray in a turned-off oven (to keep it out of the way) and it becomes very stale in a week (of course, take it out when you need to use the oven).

Linguine with Hake in Anchovy Sauce

One beautiful, late summer day I was visiting my friends Professor Sidney Mintz and his wife, Jackie, in Baltimore. Baltimore is one of my favorite American cities, a place where you can find very good soft-shell crabs in season and fresh fish such as the hake we used to make this preparation. It was a perfect meal al fresco, accompanied with a salad of roasted bell peppers. Jackie made a plum compote recipe from our mutual friend Deborah Madison's cookbook, washed down with a splendid dessert wine.

MAKES 6 SERVINGS

———

1½ pounds hake fillets, cut into bite-size pieces
2 large eggs, beaten
Dry bread crumbs for dredging
1½ cups olive oil
3 garlic cloves, finely chopped
¼ cup finely chopped fresh basil leaves
½ teaspoon red chili pepper flakes (optional)
1 teaspoon grated lemon zest
10 salted anchovy fillets, rinsed and patted dry
Freshly ground black pepper to taste
½ to ¾ cup extra-virgin olive oil
1¼ pounds linguine

———

1. Dip the hake pieces into the egg and then dredge in the bread crumbs. Set aside in the refrigerator for 30 minutes.

2. Meanwhile, heat the olive oil in a large skillet over medium-high heat until it is nearly smoking. Set the oven to the warm setting (150°F).

3. Remove the hake from the refrigerator and fry a few pieces at a time in the hot oil until golden brown, about 2 minutes a side, turning once. Remove, drain on paper towels, and salt immediately. Continue until all the hake is cooked. Keep warm in the oven, uncovered.

4. Place the garlic, basil, red pepper flakes, lemon zest, anchovies, and black pepper in a small skillet or saucepan with the extra-virgin olive oil. Turn the heat to medium and warm gently, never letting it bubble.

5. Meanwhile, bring a large pot of abundantly salted water to a rolling boil and add the pasta. Drain when al dente. Toss with three-quarters of the sauce, then transfer to a serving platter and scatter the fried hake on top. Spoon the remaining sauce over the hake and serve.

Grind in a food processor and store in bags. If a recipe calls for fine bread crumbs, place the dry bread crumbs in a food processor and run until fine. Many Italian markets sell bags of bread crumbs and of course you can buy them in a supermarket. If you do buy the supermarket variety, buy the plain, not the seasoned or "Italian-style," as the plain are more adaptable to my recipes. Fresh bread crumbs are made by placing fresh or day-old bread in a food processor and running until reduced to crumbs.

Linguine with Salmon

Salmon really is an extraordinary fish. Its taste is so rich and luscious that a quick dish like this linguine doesn't need much extra flavor, although I add the shrimp to give the sauce a little surprise and indulgence.

MAKES 4 SERVINGS

––––––

2 tablespoons extra-virgin olive oil
2 garlic cloves, finely chopped
1¼ pounds salmon fillets, preferably with skin removed,
cut into 1½-inch cubes
Salt and freshly ground black pepper to taste
½ cup dry white wine
4 to 6 medium-size shrimp, shelled and deveined
¾ pound linguine

––––––

1. In a large skillet, heat the olive oil over medium heat and cook the garlic for less than 1 minute, stirring constantly so it doesn't burn. Add the salmon, season with salt and pepper, and cook until the fish has turned color on all sides, about 3 minutes. Pour in the wine, add the shrimp, raise the heat to medium-high, and cook until the wine is a bit evaporated, about 5 minutes. Turn the heat off and let rest until the linguine is cooked.

2. Meanwhile, bring a large pot of salted water to a rolling boil and add the pasta. Drain when al dente and transfer to a serving bowl or platter. Ladle the salmon, shrimp, and sauce over the pasta and serve.

Tagliatelle with Scorpionfish

When you travel to Italy you must order *scorfano*, a Mediterranean fish known in English as scorpionfish. The taste and texture are extraordinary; if you've got Italians or Greeks in your neighborhood, it's possible a local fishmonger might have some air-freighted. In its place you will do very well with redfish (ocean perch), grouper, rockfish, or wolffish (ocean catfish). Feel free in step 3 to reduce the amount of olive oil for the sauce by half if you wish.

MAKES 4 TO 6 SERVINGS

————

2 cups olive oil for frying
3 garlic cloves, 1 crushed and 2 very finely chopped
1 pound scorpionfish or other suggested fish fillets, cut into
bite-size pieces
Flour for dredging
Salt to taste
1/2 yellow bell pepper, seeded and finely chopped
6 tablespoons very finely chopped fresh parsley leaves
1 teaspoon freshly ground black pepper
1/2 teaspoon cayenne pepper, or to taste
1 pound tagliatelle

————

continued

1. Heat the olive oil for frying in an electric frying pan to 375°F or in a large skillet over medium-high heat until it is nearly smoking. Add the crushed garlic to the oil and just before it begins to turn light brown, remove and discard it. Preheat the oven to 150°F.

2. Dredge the fish in the flour, tapping off any excess. Fry the fish in the olive oil until golden, about 90 seconds per side, without crowding the skillet. Remove with tongs or a slotted ladle or skimmer and place on a paper towel-lined baking tray to keep warm in the oven while you continue. Salt the fish as soon as they emerge from the oil.

3. In a small skillet, heat 10 tablespoons of the oil in which you fried the fish over medium-high heat and cook the yellow pepper, chopped garlic, parsley, and black and cayenne peppers until the yellow pepper has softened, about 2 minutes, stirring or shaking frequently.

4. Meanwhile, bring a large pot of abundantly salted water to a rolling boil and add the pasta. Drain when al dente. Toss with the sauce in the skillet, place the fish on top, and serve.

Linguine with Red Snapper in
Tomato Basil Sauce

*W*hen a platter of linguine, fresh tomato, basil, and garlic is this effortless, I am mightily pleased. And the glistening red skin of the fish is so appetizing.

MAKES 4 SERVINGS

———

4 red snapper fillets (about 3/4 pound total)
All-purpose flour for dredging
Milk for dipping
Dry bread crumbs for dredging
3/4 cup olive oil
Salt to taste
2 large, ripe tomatoes (about 3/4 pound), peeled, seeded, and chopped
1/4 cup finely chopped fresh basil leaves
2 garlic cloves, chopped
Freshly ground black pepper to taste
3/4 pound linguine

———

1. Preheat the oven to 150°F. Dredge the snapper fillets in the flour, tapping off any excess. Dip in the milk and dredge in the bread crumbs. Set aside on a plate in the refrigerator while you continue the preparation.

2. Heat the olive oil in a large skillet over medium-high heat until it is nearly smoking. Fry the snapper fillets until golden, about 2 minutes per side, and remove with a spatula or tongs to a paper towel-

lined baking tray, salt immediately, and keep warm in the oven. Turn the heat off under the skillet but leave the oil.

3. After the frying oil has cooled for 2 minutes, add the tomatoes, basil, and garlic, season with salt and pepper, and leave for 5 minutes with the heat off, stirring occasionally.

4. Meanwhile, bring a large pot of abundantly salted water to a rolling boil and add the pasta. Drain when al dente. Toss the pasta with the sauce in the skillet. Transfer to a serving platter and lay the red snapper fillets on top. Serve immediately.

Perciatelli with Fried Oysters and Fresh Herb Pesto

I love the pungent flavors of this garlic and red pepper-enhanced pesto made with three aromatic herbs: parsley, mint, and coriander. It is a very satisfying main course, somewhat exotic, but colorful and delicious. I normally make pesto with a mortar and pestle (that's why they call it "pesto"). One can also make it in a food processor or blender, but I find the result a little more . . . well, processed.

MAKES 2 SERVINGS

———

4 garlic cloves, peeled
1 teaspoon salt
¹/₄ cup finely chopped fresh parsley leaves
¹/₄ cup finely chopped fresh mint leaves
¹/₄ cup finely chopped fresh coriander (cilantro) leaves
1 tablespoon pine nuts
¹/₄ teaspoon red chili pepper
¹/₄ cup plus 3 tablespoons extra-virgin olive oil
8 to 10 shucked oysters, drained
1 cup dry bread crumbs
Pinch of salt
¹/₂ pound perciatelli
Freshly ground black pepper to taste

———

1. In a mortar, pound the garlic cloves and salt together with a pestle until mushy. Add the parsley, mint, coriander, pine nuts, and red

pepper and continue pounding until the herbs are no longer leafy. Continue pounding while you add 3 tablespoons of the olive oil, 1 tablespoon at a time, until the mixture achieves the consistency of a pesto—that is, very mushy.

2. Heat the remaining ¼ cup olive oil in a frying pan over medium-high heat until nearly smoking. Meanwhile, toss the oysters in a bowl with the bread crumbs and salt. Shake any excess bread crumbs off the oysters and fry until golden, about 2 minutes per side, turning once. Remove with a slotted ladle and drain on paper towels.

3. Meanwhile, bring a large pot of abundantly salted water to a rolling boil and add the pasta. Drain when al dente. Toss the pasta gently with the pesto in a large serving bowl and arrange the fried oysters on top. Grind abundant fresh pepper over the pasta and serve.

Linguine with Garlicky Fried Oysters

This is probably my favorite pasta dish. It's even better when some-one makes it for me. Once I was in San Francisco visiting my friend Carlo Middione, the chef and owner of Vivande restaurant. I arrived very tired after a long flight and he served me this dish, not knowing it was my favorite.

MAKES 4 SERVINGS

———

32 shucked oysters, drained
1/2 cup dry bread crumbs
1 cup all-purpose flour
1 teaspoon salt
6 cups olive oil for frying
5 tablespoons extra-virgin olive oil
4 garlic cloves, finely chopped
1/4 cup finely chopped fresh parsley leaves
1 pound linguine

———

1. Dredge the oysters in the bread crumbs, flour, and salt, tapping off any excess. Set aside in the refrigerator until needed.

2. Meanwhile, heat the frying oil in a deep fryer to 375°F or in an 8-inch saucepan over medium-high heat until almost smoking, about 10 minutes. Preheat the oven to 150°F.

3. In a small skillet, heat the extra-virgin olive oil over medium-high heat with the garlic and parsley. Once small bubbles begin to appear, leave for 30 seconds, then remove from the burner. Set aside.

continued

4. Deep-fry the oysters until golden brown, about 2 to 3 minutes total, turning once. Drain on paper towels set on a platter and keep warm in the oven.

5. Meanwhile, bring a large pot of abundantly salted water to a rolling boil and add the pasta. Drain when al dente. Toss the pasta with the olive oil from the small skillet and transfer to a serving platter. Arrange the oysters around the edge of the serving platter and serve. Let the frying oil cool, then strain and save.

Linguine with Garlicky Fried Soft-Shelled Clams

This is a wee bit different from the previous recipe, but just as flavorful. Soft-shelled clams, or steamers, are easy to shuck because they don't shut tight. There is something noble about oysters and something plebeian about soft-shelled steamer clams; steamers can be brinier and more reminiscent of the seashore. Then again, I'm writing this overlooking a cove at low tide in Cape Cod, the clammers stooped over in the distance, the last golden rays of sunshine sparkling in tidal pools, having just finished my last bite of this memorable linguine.

MAKES 4 SERVINGS

———

2 pounds soft-shelled clams, scrubbed, shucked, and drained
of their juices
1 cup fine dry bread crumbs

Salt to taste
1 cup olive oil
3 tablespoons finely chopped fresh parsley leaves
2 garlic cloves, finely chopped
4 salted anchovy fillets, rinsed, patted dry, and chopped
½ pound linguine
Freshly ground black pepper to taste

———

1. Dredge the clams in the bread crumbs and salt, shake off any excess bread crumbs, and set aside on a tray in the refrigerator until needed.

2. Heat the olive oil in a large skillet over medium-high heat until the oil almost begins to smoke, about 10 minutes. Carefully slip the clams into the hot oil, taking care not to crowd the pan. Cook in 2 batches if necessary. Shake the pan as you cook the clams until they are golden and crispy, 2 to 3 minutes, turning with long tongs if necessary. Add the parsley, garlic, and anchovies and cook for another 15 seconds.

3. Meanwhile, bring a large pot of abundantly salted water to a rolling boil and add the pasta. Drain when al dente. Transfer the linguine to a serving platter or individual pasta bowls, ladle the fried clams on top with a small amount of olive oil, and serve with a generous grinding of black pepper.

Linguine with Clam and Squid Sauce

I have a zillion versions of this classic linguine in white clam sauce. It's a dish that appears on every Italian-American restaurant menu, too often made with canned chopped clams. Well, say good-bye to those cans because here's the real thing. Although both fresh and frozen squid are now often sold cleaned, you may need to clean your own—it's fun though. Pull the tentacles, head, and any attached viscera, including the quill-shaped cartilage, from the body. Cut the tentacles off below the eyes. Pinch the purple skin from the body and peel off. Wash the body inside and out and the tentacles, too.

MAKES 2 TO 4 SERVINGS

———

¹/₃ cup extra-virgin olive oil
6 squid (about ³/₄ pound), cleaned and sliced into rings
3 or 4 large garlic cloves, to your taste, finely chopped
1 large dried red chili pepper, crumbled
Salt and freshly ground black pepper to taste
18 littleneck clams, scrubbed
¹/₂ pound linguine
3 tablespoons finely chopped fresh parsley leaves

———

1. In a large skillet or casserole, heat the olive oil over medium-high heat and cook the squid, garlic, red pepper, salt, and pepper for 2 minutes, stirring. Add the clams, cover, and cook until they open wider, about 10 minutes.

2. Meanwhile, bring a large pot of abundantly salted water to a rolling boil and add the pasta. Drain when al dente. Transfer the

pasta to a serving platter. Remove the opened clams and arrange over the pasta. Discard any clams that have not opened. Stir the parsley into the sauce and ladle over the pasta, using as much or as little of it as you like.

Spaghetti with Crab Diavolo Sauce

My good friend Boyd Grove doesn't cook, but he loves to eat. He gave me the idea for this dish when I fruitlessly lectured him about how easy it is to cook. I told him that you start with an idea—for instance, a taste you crave. Being from Baltimore, Boyd naturally loves spicy crabs. So here's a sauce that Boyd may never cook but you certainly can whip up as fast as the devil.

MAKES 4 SERVINGS

———

1/4 to 1/2 cup extra-virgin olive oil
1 small onion, finely chopped
4 garlic cloves, finely chopped
1/4 cup finely chopped fresh parsley leaves
2 cups canned crushed tomatoes
1 teaspoon cayenne pepper
Salt and freshly ground black pepper to taste
1/2 pound cooked crabmeat, picked over for shells and cartilage
1 pound spaghetti

———

continued

CRAB

∼

Although there are several species of crabs, only a few are commercially available. The most convenient way to use crab is to buy already picked and cleaned fresh crabmeat. This is not canned, but sold in the fresh fish sections of supermarkets and by good fishmongers. The markets usually sell two kinds of picked and cleaned crabmeat: lump crabmeat, which consists of choice pieces of meat and is expensive; and backfin, which is smaller pieces of meat. Backfin crab is perfectly fine for the recipes in this book.

∼

1. Heat 2 to 4 tablespoons of the olive oil in a large skillet over medium-high heat and cook the onion, garlic, and parsley until the onion is translucent, 5 to 6 minutes, stirring frequently so the garlic doesn't burn. Add the tomatoes and cayenne pepper, season with salt and black pepper, reduce the heat to medium-low, and cook until dense, about 15 minutes. Add the crabmeat and mix well. Leave over medium-low heat until the pasta is cooked.

2. Meanwhile, bring a large pot of abundantly salted water to a rolling boil and add the pasta. Drain when al dente. Toss the pasta with the sauce in the skillet, then pour the remaining olive oil over the top, toss again, and serve.

Pennette with Scallops and Arugula-Basil Sauce

Pennette, the diminutive of penne, the quill-shaped pasta in the macaroni family, is tossed with scallops and a tomato topping flavored with arugula and basil. This is a delightful dish that I often make in the summer with a grilled fish steak.

MAKES 4 SERVINGS

¹/₄ cup extra-virgin olive oil
1 medium-size red onion, finely chopped
2 large garlic cloves, finely chopped
1 bunch arugula (about 6 ounces), trimmed of tough stems
2 large, ripe tomatoes (about 1 pound), peeled, seeded,
and chopped
Salt and freshly ground black pepper to taste
³/₄ pound fresh bay scallops
20 large fresh basil leaves
³/₄ pound pennette

---

1. Heat the olive oil in a large skillet or casserole over medium-high heat and cook the onion and garlic until they start to color, about 2 minutes, stirring constantly so the garlic doesn't burn. Add the arugula and stir until it wilts, about 1 minute. Add the tomatoes, season with salt and pepper, and cook until some juice has evaporated, about 5 minutes. Add the scallops and cook until firm, about 4 minutes. Add the basil and let it wilt, about 1 minute, stirring all the time.

2. Meanwhile, bring a large pot of abundantly salted water to a rolling boil and add the pasta. Drain when al dente. Toss with the sauce in the skillet and serve with a grinding of black pepper.

Spaghetti with Shrimp and Scallops

The velvety taste of this superb dish cannot but help you feel better. The taste goes right to that little spot in your brain that says "perfect flavor." In addition, it is fast and easy. Vary the amount of olive oil used to your taste.

MAKES 4 SERVINGS

---

1 pound medium-size shrimp

2 cups water

1 pound bay scallops

6 to 12 tablespoons extra-virgin olive oil

6 tablespoons dry white wine

Salt and freshly ground black pepper to taste

¹/₄ teaspoon dried oregano

¹/₈ teaspoon cayenne pepper

¹/₂ cup very finely chopped onion

2 garlic cloves, finely chopped

6 ripe plum tomatoes, peeled, seeded, and finely chopped

2 tablespoons very finely chopped fresh basil leaves

³/₄ pound spaghetti

---

1. Peel the shrimp and put the shells in a small saucepan with the water. Bring to a boil, then reduce the heat to low and let simmer while you continue working.

2. Set the peeled shrimp aside with the scallops in a bowl with half (3 to 6 tablespoons) of the olive oil, the wine, salt (unless you're on

a low-sodium diet, don't be timid with the salt—it will benefit the shrimp and not hurt anything else), pepper, oregano, and cayenne.

3. In a large skillet, heat the remaining 3 to 6 tablespoons olive oil over high heat and cook the onion and garlic for 2 minutes, stirring constantly so the garlic doesn't burn. Add the tomatoes and cook for 1 minute, shake the pan, and then pour in ½ cup of the strained shrimp broth and cook, reducing the broth for 2½ minutes, stirring frequently. Add the shrimp-and-scallop mixture and cook until they turn color and are firm, about 4 minutes, stirring. Add the basil, stir, and remove the pan from the heat. Let the sauce sit while you finish preparing the pasta.

4. Meanwhile, bring a large pot of abundantly salted water to a rolling boil and add the pasta. Drain when al dente. Transfer the pasta to a serving platter and pour the sauce over it. Let the platter sit for 5 minutes to let the flavors penetrate before serving.

Fettuccine with Shrimp, Celery, and Basil Sauce

The sauce for the fettuccine starts with a soffritto of onion, celery, garlic, and basil—a wonderful beginning for the shellfish.

MAKES 4 SERVINGS

———

1 pound medium-size shrimp
1 1/2 cups water
1/3 cup finely chopped onion
3 tablespoons finely chopped celery
1 garlic clove, finely chopped
4 teaspoons finely chopped fresh basil leaves
3 tablespoons extra-virgin olive oil
2 tablespoons unsalted butter
Salt and freshly ground black pepper to taste
1 pound fettuccine or tagliatelle

———

1. Peel the shrimp, putting the shells in a small saucepan filled with the water. Bring to a boil, then reduce the heat to low and let simmer while you continue working. Chop the shrimp and set aside.

2. Put the onion, celery, garlic, and basil in a medium-size skillet with the olive oil and butter. Turn the heat to medium-high and cook, stirring, until the vegetables are soft, 5 to 6 minutes. Add the shrimp, salt (liberally), and pepper, and cook until the shrimp turn slightly orange, about 4 minutes.

3. Strain the shrimp broth, reserving ¾ cup, and pour it into the shrimp. Stir and shake over medium-high heat, reducing the amount of liquid, about 3 minutes.

4. Meanwhile, bring a large pot of abundantly salted water to a rolling boil and add the pasta. Drain the pasta when al dente. Pour the sauce over the pasta and toss lightly. Serve immediately.

Rice

RISOTTO IS A RICE preparation typical of northern Italy. In other parts of Italy where rice is also eaten, the prepared dish is simply called *riso,* for it is not cooked by the special method used for a risotto.

My risotto recipes call for the Italian short-grain rice called Arborio, which can be found in many supermarkets today and certainly in Italian markets. If you are unable to find Arborio rice, use a short-grain Spanish rice.

The secret to a perfect risotto is the combination of two elements: a flavorful broth and the correct method of adding the broth to the rice while stirring. The goal in a risotto is to have sticky, creamy rice. Unlike with a pilaf, where you never touch the rice while it is cooking, in a risotto you are almost constantly stirring the rice. Stirring the rice distributes the starchiness that makes the creamy effect when combined with a flavorful broth.

Risotto alla Campagnolo

Risotto reaches some glorious heights in the Veneto region, where short-grain rice is cooked with the slow addition of a flavorful broth. *Alla campagnolo* means, roughly, "the way our buddies like it"—something you whip up among friends. (The usual Italian home cook's method of measuring rice is one handful per person and one handful for the pot.)

MAKES 4 SERVINGS

———

6 ounces mild Italian sausage, casings removed
1 small onion, very finely chopped
1 garlic clove, crushed
1/2 cup very finely chopped fennel bulb
1/2 cup seeded and very finely chopped red bell pepper
4 fresh sage leaves, very finely chopped
1 cup Arborio rice
4 to 6 cups vegetable broth
1/2 cup dry white wine
1/2 cup freshly grated Parmesan cheese

———

1. Crumble the sausage in a heavy-bottomed 2-quart saucepan and cook over medium heat with the onion, garlic, fennel, red pepper, and sage, stirring, until the sausage loses all its pinkness and the vegetables are soft, 5 to 6 minutes. Taste the cooked sausage to see how salty it is. If it is salty, you won't need to salt the rice later.

2. Add the rice to the saucepan and cook for 1 to 2 minutes, stirring to coat the grains with the fat. Pour in a ladleful of the broth and stir.

Once it has evaporated, pour in the wine and let it evaporate. Keep pouring in broth, about ½ cup at a time, stirring frequently, until the rice is between al dente and tender. Stir in the cheese and serve.

Risotto with Wine and Chicken Livers

If you like chopped chicken livers, you'll love this risotto with its mellow flavor of butter, wine, and sage.

MAKES 4 SERVINGS

---

1 small onion, peeled
1 tablespoon fresh parsley leaves
1 tablespoon fresh sage leaves
3 tablespoons unsalted butter
1 tablespoon extra-virgin olive oil
³/4 pound chicken livers, trimmed of membranes and chopped
1 cup Arborio rice
³/4 teaspoon salt
¹/2 cup dry white wine
2 to 4 cups chicken broth
¹/2 cup freshly grated Parmesan cheese
Freshly ground black pepper to taste

continued

1. Chop the onion, parsley, and sage together very finely. In a heavy-bottomed 2-quart saucepan, melt 2 tablespoons of the butter with the olive oil over medium heat. When the butter stops bubbling, cook the onion mixture, stirring, until softened, about 6 minutes. Add the chicken livers and cook until they turn color, about 2 minutes, stirring. Add the rice to the saucepan along with the salt and cook for 1 to 2 minutes, stirring to coat the grains with the fat. Pour in the wine, stirring and once it evaporates, pour in 1 cup of the chicken broth. Stir occasionally and once the liquid evaporates, pour in another ½ cup of broth. Continue adding liquid in smaller and smaller amounts as it evaporates and is absorbed, stirring all the time, until the rice is between al dente and tender. Stir in the remaining tablespoon butter, the cheese, and pepper. Serve immediately.

Cucumber Risotto

Cucumbers are a mild-tasting vegetable, yet they do have a subtle flavor that complements rice. In this risotto, so easy to make, butter and Parmesan cheese are added at the end of the cooking to enhance the delicate flavors.

MAKES 4 SERVINGS

———

2 tablespoons extra-virgin olive oil
2 cucumbers, peeled, seeded, and finely chopped
3 tablespoons finely chopped onion
1 large garlic clove, very finely chopped
1 cup Arborio rice
Salt and freshly and finely ground white pepper
4 to 6 cups vegetable or chicken broth
1/2 cup freshly grated Parmesan cheese
2 tablespoons unsalted butter

———

1. In a heavy-bottomed 2-quart saucepan, heat the olive oil over medium-high heat and cook the cucumbers, onion, and garlic until soft, 4 to 5 minutes, stirring occasionally. Add the rice, season with salt and pepper, and cook for 1 to 2 minutes, stirring to coat the grains with the fat. Add 1 cup of the broth, reduce the heat to medium, and cook until the liquid is absorbed. Once the liquid evaporates, pour in 1/2 cup of broth. Continue adding liquid in smaller and smaller amounts as it evaporates and is absorbed, stirring all the time, until the rice is between al dente and tender. Stir in the cheese and butter, and cook for 5 minutes or until it melts. Serve immediately.

~

Broccoli rabe is a sprouting broccoli that is also called *broccoli-rave, cime di rapa, friarelli, broccoli di foglia, broccoletti di rape,* or just *rape* or *rabe* in Italian. Sometimes, both in English and Italian, broccoli rabe refers to turnip tops. It has a strong taste, a little bitter, that improves with cooking.

~

Risotto of Crayfish, Broccoli Rabe, and Portobello Mushrooms

My supermarket had picked cooked crayfish one day, but you can use cooked lobster, shrimp, or crab. This dish is a meal in itself and very satisfying. Use homemade fish broth if you have any handy, otherwise a couple of fish bouillon cubes will do just fine, although you should remember that these cubes are salty.

MAKES 4 TO 6 SERVINGS

————

6 tablespoons (3/4 stick) unsalted butter

1 tablespoon extra-virgin olive oil

1/4 pound portobello mushroom caps (about 1 mushroom), chopped

3/4 pound broccoli rabe, tough stems removed, thoroughly washed, and chopped

2 garlic cloves, finely chopped

1 cup Arborio rice

Salt and freshly ground black pepper to taste

4 to 6 cups fish or chicken broth

1/3 pound chopped cooked crayfish, lobster, crabmeat, or shrimp

————

1. Melt 3 tablespoons of the butter with the olive oil in a heavy-bottomed 2-quart saucepan over high heat. Once the butter has stopped bubbling, cook the mushrooms, broccoli rabe, and garlic until the greens are wilted, 2 to 3 minutes, stirring constantly. Add the rice, season with salt and pepper, and cook for 1 to 2 minutes, stirring to coat the grains with the fat.

2. Pour in 1 cup of the broth, reduce the heat to medium, and continue stirring. Once the liquid evaporates, pour in another ½ cup of broth. Continue adding liquid in smaller and smaller amounts as it evaporates and is absorbed, stirring all the time, until the rice is between al dente and tender. After the last addition of liquid, stir in the shellfish and cook for another 5 minutes, stirring. Stir in the remaining 3 tablespoons butter and serve once it melts.

CHAPTER EIGHT

Meat

ONE OF THE DISTRESSING THINGS I've noticed as a home cook is the increasingly poor quality of beef in supermarkets. The labeling of beef products is shameful and supermarkets are big culprits. Once you could get either a USDA prime or choice steak without a problem. Now supermarket meat departments offer "better-read-the-fine-print" USDA select quality beef that is really not very good. Then again, it's a challenge that the Italian family cook faced every day years ago: how to cook poor-quality meat. My family eats beef so infrequently, maybe four times a month, that when we do eat it we want the best. These recipes for beef assume that you're using prime or choice quality, but remember that you may have to ask the manager for it unless you do your shopping at a meat market, the few that there are.

I wish there was a happier story to tell about pork, veal, and lamb. You still need to shop carefully. Avoid imported New Zealand lamb and stick with American lamb, which tastes much better. As for chickens, the best tasting are those nonindustrial chickens called free or semi-free range. They can often be found in supermarkets, but you may need to ask. An interesting circumstance I've stumbled across in my search for quality meats and poultry is that often there are superior-tasting products from butchers operating under Jewish or Muslim religious authorities—that is, kosher or halal meats. I haven't researched the reason for this, but you may want to give your local kosher or halal market a try.

Skillet-Fried Steak with Black, White, and Red Peppers

I think this preparation is superlative with the distinctive texture of skirt steak. If you use another kind of steak, pound it thinner first. Serve with Spaghetti with Anchovies, Herbs, and Spices (page 128). You will need to use your exhaust fan full blast to remove the smoke.

MAKES 4 SERVINGS

———

Extra-virgin olive oil for drizzling
1 1/2 teaspoons salt
1 teaspoon freshly ground black pepper
1 teaspoon freshly ground white pepper
1/2 teaspoon cayenne pepper
1 tablespoon dried oregano
1 1/2 pounds beef steak (skirt, Delmonico, or top sirloin), cut into four
1/2-inch-thick steaks and trimmed of surrounding fat

———

1. Preheat a large cast-iron skillet or griddle with a film of extra-virgin olive oil over high heat until very hot, 8 to 10 minutes. Mix the salt, peppers and oregano. Spread the spices in a plate and dredge the steaks in it on both sides.

2. Place the steaks in the hot skillet and cook about 4 to 5 minutes a side or less for very rare—a nice way to do a skirt steak.

~

Thyme is an excellent garden herb, easy to grow and maintain. Its strong and distinctive odor is wonderful in sauces or marinades, and both dried and fresh thyme are fine for use in these recipes. Use only the leaves, not the stems. Peel by running your thumb and forefinger from tip to stem base, pushing off the leaves.

~

Sear-Crusted Thyme and White Pepper Steak

I love skirt steak for this recipe, but you can use any kind—rib eye, sirloin tip, New York strip, flank, T-bone, or Porterhouse. The steak develops a delicious golden crust while searing over high heat.

MAKES 4 SERVINGS

———

2 tablespoons extra-virgin olive oil
1 garlic clove, crushed
1½ pounds beef steak, cut into four ½-inch-thick steaks and trimmed of surrounding fat
1 tablespoon dried or fresh thyme leaves
1 tablespoon freshly ground white pepper
Salt to taste

———

1. Put the oil and garlic in a large cast-iron skillet and turn the heat to high. When the garlic begins to turn light brown, remove and discard it.

2. Meanwhile, coat the steaks on both sides with the thyme, pepper, and salt. When the oil in the pan just begins to smoke, add the steaks and press down with a spatula. Cook for 4 to 5 minutes a side for rare. Remove from the pan and serve.

Flank Steak with Walnut Pesto

This pungent pesto is made with walnuts, basil, and garlic and is spread over very thin panfried flank steaks. Although it's not necessary, it is nice to butterfly the flank steak to make it thinner. Have the butcher butterfly the steak or do it yourself by placing your hand on top of the meat and cutting through with a long slicing knife, making sure that your hand does not stray in front of the cutting edge.

MAKES 4 SERVINGS

20 large fresh basil leaves
1/4 cup walnut meats
3 tablespoons freshly grated Pecorino Pepato or Pecorino cheese
5 garlic cloves, 4 whole and 1 crushed
5 to 6 tablespoons extra-virgin olive oil
Salt and freshly ground black pepper to taste
1 pound flank steak, butterflied about 1/4 inch thick, then cut into thin strips against the grain

1. Put the basil, walnuts, cheese, and 4 whole garlic cloves in a mortar and pound until a paste forms or process in a food processor or blender. Transfer to a bowl, whip in 4 to 5 tablespoons of the olive oil, and season with salt and pepper.

2. Heat the remaining tablespoon olive oil in a large cast-iron skillet over high heat with the crushed garlic clove. As the garlic begins to turn light brown, remove and discard it. Add the steak strips and cook until just browned, 1 to 2 minutes per side, and transfer to a serving platter. Cover with the pesto and serve.

Grilled Sirloin Tip, Bay Leaf, and Onion

Grilling sirloin with aromatic flavors is a nice change from a hamburger. In this preparation the steak takes on the aromas of bay leaf and onion and is flavored with a hint of balsamic vinegar. Soak the skewers in water before grilling to retard their burning.

MAKES 4 SERVINGS

———

1½ pounds sirloin tips, cubed
1 medium-size onion, peeled, quartered, and separated into layers
16 bay leaves, soaked in tepid water to cover for 30 minutes, drained, and halved
Extra-virgin olive oil to taste
Balsamic vinegar to taste
Freshly ground black pepper to taste
Dried oregano to taste
Salt to taste

———

1. Preheat a gas grill on high for 20 minutes or prepare a hot charcoal fire.

2. Skewer the meat, onion pieces, and bay leaf halves, alternating them, on six 10-inch wooden skewers. Continue until they are all used up. You should end up with 4 pieces of meat on each skewer.

3. Coat the food on each skewer with some olive oil, balsamic vinegar, pepper, and oregano. Just before grilling, salt the meat and grill for 10 to 15 minutes, or to taste. Serve immediately.

Panfried Sandwich Steaks with Tomatoes and Parsley

Many supermarkets sell thin-sliced "sandwich" steaks, usually a bottom cut of beef round. These steaks are perfect for quick-frying with some fresh tomatoes and onions. I like to keep it simple and serve this with bruschetta and perhaps a salad of greens.

MAKES 4 SERVINGS

———

1/4 cup red pepper olive oil (page 92)
2 cups chopped onions
2 cups chopped or crushed canned or fresh tomatoes
3 garlic cloves, finely chopped
3 tablespoons finely chopped fresh parsley leaves
2 pounds thinly sliced bottom round steaks
Salt and freshly ground black pepper to taste

———

1. Heat the red pepper oil in a large cast-iron skillet over medium-high heat and cook the onions until golden, about 5 minutes, stirring occasionally. Add the tomatoes, garlic, and parsley and cook, until sputtering, another 3 minutes.

2. Add the sandwich steaks to the pan with some salt and pepper and cook until browned on both sides, about 4 minutes total. Serve immediately with crusty Italian bread or bruschetta.

Baby Meatballs in Green and White Sauce

These delicious little balls of ground lamb and beef are poached in chicken broth with spinach and cream and are very versatile: you can serve this as a soup (see the note below), as a pasta topping, or on its own.

MAKES 4 SERVINGS

————

2 tablespoons extra-virgin olive oil

$^1/_2$ cup finely chopped onion

$^3/_4$ pound ground lamb

$^3/_4$ pound ground beef

Salt and freshly ground black pepper to taste

1 garlic clove, finely chopped

$^1/_2$ cup chicken broth

10 ounces fresh spinach, trimmed of tough stems, thoroughly washed, and chopped

2 tablespoons pine nuts

$^1/_2$ cup heavy cream

————

1. In a large skillet, heat the olive oil over medium-high heat and cook the onion until translucent, about 6 minutes, stirring occasionally.

2. Meanwhile, start making the meatballs by kneading the lamb, beef, salt, and pepper together with both hands in a mixing bowl. Quickly form the meatballs into walnut-size balls, keeping your hands wet with cold water so the meat doesn't stick.

3. Add the meatballs to the skillet along with the garlic and shake the pan vigorously to keep the meatballs from sticking. Once the meatballs are browned on all sides, about 5 minutes, cook them for another 3 or 4 minutes, then remove them from the pan and set aside. Discard all the accumulated fat from the skillet with a spoon or ladle.

4. Add the chicken broth, chopped spinach, and pine nuts to the skillet. Check and correct the seasonings. Reduce the heat to medium and cook until the broth is reduced by two-thirds. Return the meatballs to the skillet, add the cream, and cook until the sauce is velvety, about 5 minutes. Serve immediately with rice or a short pasta such as tubetti, elbow macaroni, or orzo.

VARIATION: To make this recipe into a soup, use 1 cup chicken broth and 1 cup cream and reduce by half, not two-thirds.

Grilled Veal Chops and Spaghettini
with Yellow Squash and Shiitake Mushrooms

Here veal chops are grilled until streaked with black grid marks and then placed on top of a bed of spaghettini tossed with vegetables. This is a complete meal, and very satisfying.

MAKES 4 SERVINGS

———

2 tablespoons extra-virgin olive oil

3 ounces fresh shiitake mushrooms, cut in half if large
and stems discarded

$1/2$ cup dry white wine

1 yellow summer squash, thinly sliced

3 tablespoons finely chopped fresh basil leaves

2 garlic cloves, finely chopped

Salt and freshly ground black pepper to taste

$3/4$ pound spaghettini

$1/3$ cup fresh or frozen peas

3 tablespoons freshly grated Pecorino cheese

4 veal chops, cut in half, or 4 thin chops (about $3/4$ to 1 pound)

———

1. Prepare a hot charcoal fire or preheat a gas grill on high for 20 minutes.

2. Heat the olive oil in a large skillet over medium heat. Cook the mushrooms until softened, about 2 minutes, stirring. Add the wine and reduce for 10 minutes. Add the squash, basil, and garlic, season with salt and pepper, stir, and cook until the squash is tender, an-

other 5 minutes. Reduce the heat to very low and simmer while you prepare the veal and pasta.

3. Bring a large pot of abundantly salted water to a rolling boil, and add the pasta. After 5 minutes, add the peas. Drain when the pasta is al dente, transfer to the skillet, and toss well with the vegetables and cheese.

4. Meanwhile, lightly oil the veal chops, season with salt and pepper, and grill for 5 minutes without touching, moving, or poking the chop. Turn over onto the other side and grill another 5 minutes, again not moving them.

5. Arrange the spaghettini on a serving platter or individual plates. Place the veal chops on top and serve.

Veal Liver with Scallions and Marsala

The most important thing to remember when cooking liver is that overcooked liver will only remind you of why you hated it as a child: overcooked liver tastes like shoe leather. Liver is delicate and requires quick, hot cooking, literally tossed in a pan for a few minutes.

MAKES 4 SERVINGS

———

5 tablespoons unsalted butter
12 scallions, white parts only, finely chopped
3 garlic cloves, finely chopped
³/4 cup finely chopped fresh parsley leaves
1 pound veal liver, trimmed of arteries and cut into ¹/2-inch cubes
³/4 cup dry Marsala wine
Salt and freshly ground black pepper to taste

———

1. Melt the butter in a large skillet over medium-high heat and once it has stopped bubbling, cook the scallions, garlic, and parsley until softened, 2 to 3 minutes, stirring.

2. Add the liver and sear for 1 to 2 minutes per side, then add the Marsala, scrape the bottom of the pan of any browned bits, season with salt and pepper, cover, and cook for 3 minutes. Remove the liver, arrange on a serving platter, and cover with the sauce.

Very Quick Venetian-Style Liver

This isn't exactly the way they do it in Venice because this recipe has no thinly sliced onions. But it is very flavorful and requires only the shortest of cooking times. Marinating in milk might seem unusual, but it is a great way to lessen the sometimes powerful taste of liver.

MAKES 4 SERVINGS

———

1 pound veal liver, trimmed of arteries
Milk
1/4 cup extra-virgin olive oil
Salt and freshly ground black pepper
Finely chopped fresh parsley leaves (optional)

———

1. Slice the veal into 2-inch lengths about an 1/8 inch thick. Place the liver in milk to cover and soak for 30 minutes to 1 hour in refrigerator.

2. Heat the olive oil in a large cast-iron skillet until it is almost smoking. Drain the liver, pat dry, season with salt and pepper, and cook, tossing constantly for 2 minutes. Remove to a serving platter and sprinkle with parsley if desired.

Costalette alla Milanese

This is the way they cook veal or pork chops in Milan and many other places. In Spanish-speaking countries you'll find them called *milanesa* and in Austria they're a "Vienna cut," better known as Wienerschnitzel. Whatever you call them, golden-crusted breaded pork or veal chops are always a favorite with my family. They are quite nice with Fennel Gratinate (page 243) and Griddled Potato Crispelle with Salmon Caviar and Mascarpone (page 250).

MAKES 4 SERVINGS

½ cup olive oil
1 pound veal or pork chops (6 to 7 chops), boned, trimmed of fat, and pounded thin
All-purpose flour for dredging
2 large eggs, beaten
Dry bread crumbs for dredging
Salt and freshly ground black pepper to taste
Lemon wedges (optional) for garnish

---

1. Heat the olive oil in a large cast-iron skillet over medium-high heat until nearly smoking, about 10 minutes.

2. Meanwhile, dredge the meat in the flour, tapping off any excess, then dip in the eggs. Dredge in the bread crumbs to evenly coat.

3. Cook the chops in the hot oil for 3 to 4 minutes per side. Do not crowd the skillet; cook in batches and keep them warm in a low oven, if necessary. Remove to a paper towel-lined tray to drain, then

transfer to a serving platter. Season with salt and pepper and serve with a wedge of lemon, if desired.

VARIATION #1: Serve the chops with caper sauce. Chop 2 tablespoons drained capers and mix with ½ cup extra-virgin olive oil and the juice of 1 lemon. Stir well and taste, correct the seasonings if necessary, and serve over the chops.

VARIATION #2: Use turkey cutlets.

Pork Chops and Golden Onions

This recipe calls for thinly sliced pork chops to be cooked over high heat for a delicious meal in almost seconds. Pork can be quite lean these days, making it an ideal family preparation. The onions and wine, cooked until they are golden and spread over the golden brown pork chops, really add a lot of flavor.

MAKES 2 SERVINGS

———

2 tablespoons unsalted butter or extra-virgin olive oil
1 medium-size onion, thinly sliced
1 pound thinly cut pork chops (about six ^{1}/4-inch-thick chops),
trimmed of fat
Salt and freshly ground black pepper to taste
^{1}/2 cup dry white wine

———

1. Heat the butter in a large skillet over high heat. When the butter stops bubbling, cook the onion until golden, about 6 minutes, stirring constantly.

2. Add the pork chops, season with salt and pepper, and cook for 1 minute on each side. Pour in the wine. Once it evaporates, serve immediately.

Lamb with Mushrooms and Onions

A succulent lamb and earthy mushrooms seem to me to be one of those natural combinations. For some reason my family wants this preparation only in the winter.

MAKES 2 SERVINGS

———

2 tablespoons extra-virgin olive oil
2 garlic cloves, crushed
1 medium-size onion, peeled, quartered, and separated into layers
1/2 pound mushrooms, sliced
1 pound lamb, cut from the loin or leg, trimmed of fat and cut into small cubes
1 tablespoon tomato paste
1 cup dry red wine
Salt and freshly ground black pepper to taste
Finely chopped fresh parsley leaves for garnish

———

1. Heat the olive oil in a large skillet or casserole and cook the garlic until it just begins to turn brown. Remove the garlic and discard.

2. Add the onion and cook over medium-high heat until translucent, about 4 minutes, stirring. Add the mushrooms and lamb and cook until the lamb is browned on all sides, about 5 minutes. Dissolve the tomato paste in the wine and pour into the pan, then season with salt and pepper and cook until the wine evaporates, about 20 minutes. Transfer to a serving platter, sprinkle with parsley, and serve.

Spezzatino of Chicken with Peppers

A *spezzatino* is an Italian family stew. I know third-generation Italian Americans who don't know a word of Italian, nor a thing about Italian culture, but they'll tell you all about their grandmother's spezzatino. These stews are made by every family, and they're all different. This recipe is a quick one that I make with chicken breast cut into fingers, a little bell pepper, onion, tomato, and some wine. When I have more time I use chicken pieces on the bone, which are more flavorful.

MAKES 4 SERVINGS

———

1 tablespoon extra-virgin olive oil
3 tablespoons unsalted butter
1 small onion, coarsely chopped
1/2 green bell pepper, seeded and coarsely chopped
1/4 cup chopped pancetta
1 garlic clove, finely chopped
1/2 cup dry white wine
1 cup chopped canned or fresh tomatoes
1 pound boneless chicken breasts, skin removed and cut into fingers
Salt and freshly ground black pepper to taste

———

1. Heat the olive oil and butter together in a large skillet or casserole over medium heat until the butter stops bubbling. Cook the onion, bell pepper, pancetta, and garlic until golden, about 12 minutes, stirring occasionally.

2. Pour in the wine and reduce for a few minutes. Add the tomatoes and cook until sputtering, about 5 minutes, stirring. Add the chicken, season with salt and pepper, and cook until cooked all the way through, about 35 minutes. Serve.

Involtini of Chicken with Ricotta

Involtini are stuffed roll-ups of meat or chicken, a popular Italian family cooking method to make meat go further. Cooked to a deep golden, these rolled-up chicken breasts look delicious. And with a dollop of creamy ricotta cheese, they are spectacular.

MAKES 4 TO 6 SERVINGS

1/2 cup dry bread crumbs
1 tablespoon finely chopped onion
1 small garlic clove, finely chopped
1 teaspoon pine nuts
1 teaspoon golden raisins
Salt and freshly ground black pepper to taste
8 boneless chicken breast halves (about 2 pounds), skin removed
2 tablespoons extra-virgin olive oil
1/2 cup ricotta cheese diluted with 2 to 3 tablespoons milk

continued

1. In a small bowl, mix the stuffing of bread crumbs, onion, garlic, pine nuts, raisins, salt, and pepper.

2. Between 2 sheets of waxed paper, flatten the chicken breast halves with a mallet or the side of a heavy cleaver until about ⅛ inch thick, making sure you don't break through the skin. Place about 1 tablespoon of the stuffing on each breast and roll up, fastening both ends closed with toothpicks if necessary. Season each roll-up with salt and pepper.

3. Heat the olive oil in a large skillet over medium heat and cook the roll-ups, turning frequently, until all the sides are a rich, deep golden brown, about 20 minutes. Arrange the chicken on a serving platter, spoon a tablespoon of ricotta cheese over each breast, and serve.

Chicken and Spinach

This is a secret way of getting kids to eat vegetables. Supermarkets usually sell shredded carrots at their salad bars and these work well in this recipe, as they save a lot of preparation time.

MAKES 4 SERVINGS

———

3 tablespoons extra-virgin olive oil
2 garlic cloves, finely chopped
$1/2$ cup finely chopped or shredded carrots
1 red bell pepper, seeded and chopped
$1^1/4$ pounds boneless chicken breasts, skin removed and cut into cubes
$1/4$ teaspoon ground cinnamon
Salt and freshly ground black pepper to taste
$1/4$ cup dry white wine
10 ounces fresh spinach, trimmed of tough stems, thoroughly washed, and shredded

———

1. Heat the olive oil in a large skillet over medium-high heat and cook the garlic for less than 1 minute. Add the carrots and red pepper, and cook for 2 to 3 minutes, stirring. Add the chicken and cinnamon, season with salt and pepper, and cook for 1 minute, then add the wine and spinach. Cook until the wine has evaporated and the spinach wilted, 5 to 6 minutes. Continue folding the spinach into the skillet as it wilts. Serve.

Baked Thyme Chicken with
Roast Potatoes and Fried Peppers

This is a meal my three kids can't stop eating—and if you have kids you know what a compliment that is. Everything cooks in about 45 minutes, so remember to start steps 2, 3, and 4 at the same time.

MAKES 4 TO 6 SERVINGS

———

3 baking potatoes (about 1 1/2 pounds), peeled and cut into
1/2-inch cubes
2 tablespoons melted duck fat (preferably, otherwise olive oil)
Salt to taste
6 boneless chicken breast halves (about 2 pounds), skin removed
1/4 cup extra-virgin olive oil
1 tablespoon dried thyme
Freshly ground black pepper to taste
2 red bell peppers, seeded and cut into strips
2 green bell peppers, seeded and cut into strips
2 light green cubanelle peppers, seeded and cut into strips
1 garlic clove, crushed

———

1. Preheat the oven to 450°F.

2. Dry the potatoes well with a paper towel. Toss them with the duck fat and salt. Arrange in a single layer in a baking pan and roast for 45 minutes. When the potatoes are half cooked, turn them with a spatula, scraping and lifting gently.

3. Toss the chicken with 1 tablespoon of the olive oil and the thyme, and season with salt and pepper. Arrange in a lightly oiled baking pan and place in the oven next to the potatoes. Bake until the potatoes and chicken are golden brown, about 45 minutes. Remove the chicken if it is cooking faster than the potatoes. The chicken will be slightly springy to the touch when it's done.

4. Meanwhile, heat the remaining 3 tablespoons olive oil in a large skillet and cook the peppers and garlic over medium-high heat until nearly smoking. Reduce the heat to medium and cook until the peppers are sizzling and the edges are curling, about 10 minutes, stirring. Reduce the heat to low and cook until soft, 45 minutes. Serve the peppers separately from the chicken and potatoes.

Chicken Scallopine with Artichoke Sauce

This elegant preparation for thin scallopine of chicken breasts uses a creamy sauce with a subtle hint of artichokes and lemon. The sauce can be made in the food processor while the chicken cooks.

MAKES 2 TO 4 SERVINGS

———

4 cooked small artichoke hearts (fresh, canned, or frozen and defrosted)
5 tablespoons mascarpone cheese
2 tablespoons heavy cream
Salt and freshly ground black pepper to taste
1/2 teaspoon freshly squeezed lemon juice
2 tablespoons extra-virgin olive oil
1 tablespoon unsalted butter
4 boneless chicken breast halves (about 1 pound), skin removed
1/4 cup dry white wine
1 tablespoon finely chopped fresh mint leaves (optional)

———

1. Put the artichoke hearts, mascarpone, and cream in a food processor or blender and blend until creamy soft, scraping down the sides if necessary. Transfer to a bowl, season with salt and pepper, and stir in the lemon juice. Set aside.

2. Pound the chicken pieces between 2 sheets of waxed paper with the side of a heavy cleaver or a mallet until about 1/8 inch thick.

3. Heat the olive oil with the butter over high heat in a large skillet. When the butter starts to bubble, cook the chicken on each side for

1 minute. Pour in the wine and continue cooking over high heat until it has nearly evaporated. Add the artichoke sauce, reduce the heat to low, and simmer gently, stirring the chicken and sauce to blend, for 6 to 8 minutes. Serve immediately with plain boiled rice and sprinkle both with the mint, if desired.

NOTE: If you are using a fresh artichoke, boil until tender and also scrape the flesh off the bracts.

Chicken with Three Onions

*D*elicate chicken breasts are cooked with onions, shallots, and scallions, while the chili peppers provide a spicy kick, but not too strong because you will discard them after cooking.

For the best result, cook this dish in a very hot skillet, preferably made of blue steel, or in a cast-iron skillet that has been preheated. Serve with rice.

MAKES 4 SERVINGS

———

¹/₄ cup extra-virgin olive oil
1 large onion, sliced
6 large shallots, sliced
9 scallions, white parts only, chopped
6 dried red chili peppers
1³/₄ pounds boneless chicken breast halves, skin removed, pounded ¹/₄
inch thick between 2 sheets of waxed paper
Salt and freshly ground black pepper to taste
Dried oregano to taste

———

1. Heat the olive oil in a skillet over very high heat. Cook the onion, shallots, scallions, and red chili peppers until softened, 3 to 4 minutes, stirring or shaking constantly. Add the chicken and continue cooking until golden brown on both sides, stirring or shaking constantly, 6 to 7 minutes. Sprinkle with salt, pepper, and oregano to taste. If the chicken is sticking, add a few tablespoons of water to the pan. When the chicken is golden brown and springy to the touch, remove and discard the chili peppers and serve.

Chicken Saltimbocca

Saltimbocca, which means "jump-in-the-mouth," is a famous preparation from Rome made with veal scallopine. In this recipe you fire up the oven instead of a skillet. The mellow taste of chicken is perfect with Broccoliflower with Bagna Cauda (page 248).

MAKES 4 SERVINGS

———

Extra-virgin olive oil
1¹/₂ pounds boneless chicken breast halves, skin removed and pounded
¹/₈ inch thick between 2 sheets of waxed paper
Salt and freshly ground black pepper to taste
¹/₂ pound fresh mozzarella, sliced
¹/₄ cup finely chopped fresh basil leaves
8 salted anchovy fillets, rinsed, patted dry, and chopped
¹/₂ cup ricotta cheese, preferably fresh

———

1. Preheat the oven to 475°F.

2. Lightly oil a large baking pan. Lay the chicken in the pan and season with salt and pepper. Cover with the mozzarella slices. Sprinkle with the basil and anchovies. Cover evenly with the ricotta cheese and place in the oven until the cheese has melted and is bubbling slightly, about 15 minutes. Remove from the oven and serve.

CHAPTER NINE

Seafood

OVER THE YEARS in my cookbooks, cooking classes, and conversation, I have dispensed a lot of advice about recognizing fresh fish. Nevertheless I find that most people still can't figure out when fish is really fresh, short of eating it. And even then I've heard them say that they don't like that particular fish instead of saying "this fish isn't fresh." It finally occurred to me that chefs, cookbook writers, and cooking teachers overemphasize recognizing fresh *whole* fish, when the likelihood of a modern American consumer finding whole fish is minimal. Nearly all fish sold today in supermarkets, and even most fish stores, are fish fillets. Because it's impossible to tell by look or smell (because of sodium benzoate) whether a fish fillet is fresh, my recommendation is to look for a quality fishmonger whom you can trust and who sells nothing but top-quality fresh fish, which you will be able to tell because it tastes great. If a fish doesn't "taste" magnificent that is very probably because it's not fresh, not because of the particular species you're eating (although fish *do* taste different). In selecting a store, look for premises that either have no smell or have a slight briny ocean smell, never a "fishy" smell, which indicates that the fish are not fresh. If you're in a fish store or supermarket fish section and your nose is beginning to turn up, leave.

Because Americans generally don't cook and eat fish, look for a fish store whose clientele is Italian, Greek, Haitian, Vietnamese, Chinese, Japanese (who have a very high appreciation for fresh fish), or other cultures with good fish cookery. Go to the fish market and buy the freshest fish, and then look for a recipe, rather than vice versa. No matter what fish I call for in a recipe, feel free to replace it with another fresh fish of the same category—for example, firm-fleshed with firm-fleshed, flaky with flaky.

Grilled Breaded Swordfish

Pure and simple magnificence. That's the only way I can describe this easy preparation. Swordfish is in season from midsummer to early fall, and that's when this recipe gets made a lot. You can pan-fry or broil the fish, too, but I prefer grilling.

MAKES 4 SERVINGS

———

¹/₂ cup dry bread crumbs
1 teaspoon dried oregano
¹/₄ teaspoon salt
¹/₈ teaspoon freshly ground black pepper
2 teaspoons freshly grated Caciocavallo or Pecorino cheese
4 swordfish steaks (1¹/₄ pounds total), skin removed
All-purpose flour for dredging
1 large egg, beaten
Extra-virgin olive oil for drizzling

———

1. Prepare a charcoal fire or preheat a gas grill on high for 20 minutes. Mix the bread crumbs, oregano, salt, pepper, and cheese on a plate.

2. Dredge the swordfish in the flour and tap off any excess. Dip in the egg on both sides, then dredge again in the bread crumb mixture, coating evenly.

3. Drizzle the top of the swordfish with olive oil. Place the oiled side down on the grill and cook for 4 minutes. Flip to the other side and grill another 4 minutes. Serve immediately.

Baked Swordfish with Oregano
and Anchovy Crust

Swordfish is incredibly popular in Sicily, from where my recipe is inspired. The best months for swordfish are July, August, and September. This recipe is best made on a cool, late September day.

MAKES 4 SERVINGS

———

*One 2-pound swordfish steak, at least 3/4 inch thick but not more than
1 inch thick, skin removed*
3/4 cup dry bread crumbs
8 salted anchovy fillets, rinsed, patted dry, and finely chopped
2 garlic cloves, finely chopped
2 tablespoons dried oregano
2 tablespoons finely chopped fresh parsley leaves
1/4 cup extra-virgin olive oil
Salt and freshly ground black pepper to taste
Extra-virgin olive oil for drizzling
Finely chopped fresh parsley leaves for garnish

———

1. Cut the swordfish into 4 pieces. Slice each piece in half horizontally with a sharp slicing knife, keeping the pieces matched.

2. Mix the bread crumbs, anchovies, garlic, oregano, and parsley and moisten with the olive oil. This bread crumb coating should look like wet sand.

3. Preheat the oven to 425°F. Lightly oil a 12 × 9-inch baking pan with 1- to 2-inch sides. Arrange the bottom pieces of the swordfish

in the pan and coat them with half the bread crumb mixture. Lightly season with salt and pepper. Layer the top pieces of swordfish over the bread crumb coating and lightly salt and pepper again. Spread the remaining bread crumb mixture over the top layer of swordfish. Drizzle a little olive oil over the top and place in the oven until the crust is golden brown and crunchy looking, and the fish is springy to the touch, 15 to 20 minutes. Remove the pan from the oven, transfer to a serving platter, sprinkle with parsley, and serve.

Grilled Skewers of
Swordfish and Orange

I make this *spitini,* a Sicilian-style shish kebab, in August or September when I just can't get enough swordfish. Don't peel the oranges—you eat them, too. It's so good. Soak the skewers in water to retard their burning.

MAKES 4 TO 6 SERVINGS

———

1 medium-size onion, peeled, quartered, and separated into layers
1¹/₂ pounds swordfish steaks, skin removed and cut into
1-inch cubes
2 oranges, cut into small cubes and seeded
12 small or 6 large bay leaves, soaked in tepid water to cover for 10
minutes and drained
Salt and freshly ground black pepper to taste
Extra-virgin olive oil for dipping and drizzling
Dry bread crumbs for dredging

———

1. Prepare a hot charcoal fire or preheat a gas grill on high for 20 minutes.

2. Double-skewer all the ingredients: hold 2 skewers parallel to each other about ¹/₂ inch apart between your thumb and forefinger. Skewer an onion, a piece of swordfish, a piece of orange, and a bay leaf, in that order. Repeat until all the ingredients are skewered. You should have 4 pieces of onion, 4 pieces of swordfish, 3 pieces of orange, and 2 bay leaves per double skewer. Break the bay leaves in

half if large. The double skewer keeps the ingredients from sliding and helps them cook more evenly. Season with salt and pepper.

3. Dip each double skewer in a platter filled with a little olive oil, then dredge in the bread crumbs. Drizzle a tiny bit of olive oil over each skewer before placing on the grill for 4 minutes a side. Serve on the skewer.

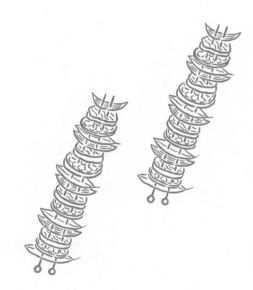

Broiled Shark with Pesto Trapanese

*O*n the western coast of Sicily, the port of Trapani is famous for seafood preparations, especially tuna, but also for a shark called *palombo* (dogfish). Up and down the coast in small hamlets cooks make this sauce, calling it a Trapani-style pesto to mimic the famous pesto of Genoa made with basil, pine nuts, and Parmesan. In my recipe I use shark, a great-tasting fish seen more and more in the market, otherwise this dish can be made with swordfish. Be absolutely sure your tomatoes are drained completely, otherwise the pesto will be watery. Serve with a side dish of Spinach and Fresh Ricotta Gratinate (page 235).

MAKES 4 SERVINGS

———

4 garlic cloves, peeled
25 large fresh basil leaves
3 tablespoons ground roasted almonds
3/4 pounds ripe tomatoes, peeled, seeded, and very well drained
Salt and freshly ground black pepper to taste
3 tablespoons extra-virgin olive oil
Four 1/2-inch-thick shark steaks (11/2 pounds total)
1 tablespoon chopped imported black olives (optional)
1 tablespoon chopped imported green olives (optional)
5 tablespoons dry bread crumbs

———

1. Preheat the broiler.

2. Pound the garlic, basil, almonds, tomatoes, salt, and pepper in a mortar or process using short pulses in a food processor or blender

until a paste forms, scraping down the sides, then slowly add the olive oil in a trickle. Check the seasonings.

3. Lightly oil a broiler pan. Arrange the shark slices on the pan and season with salt and pepper. Spread the pesto on top, with the olives, if using. Cover with the bread crumbs and place under the broiler until the bread crumbs begin to form black specks, about 12 minutes. Serve immediately.

Grilled Salmon with Artichoke, Oyster, and Rosemary Sauce on Lingue

Artichokes are as noble a vegetable as salmon is a fish. This *piatto unico* (one-platter meal) subtly combines four distinctive flavors: artichokes, oysters, salmon, and rosemary. Very little olive oil is used; the flavor comes from these four ingredients. I use lingue, a flat pasta wider than linguine but narrower than fettuccine.

MAKES 2 SERVINGS

———

1 tablespoon extra-virgin olive oil

1/4 cup very finely chopped onion

2 garlic cloves, finely chopped

2 cooked artichoke hearts, very thinly sliced

3 tablespoons dry white wine

1 cup fish broth

1 sprig fresh rosemary

3 to 5 oysters (about 1/2 pound), shucked with their liquor

Salt and freshly ground black pepper to taste

3/4 pound salmon fillets, cut from the thickest section into 2 or 3 equal pieces, each about 1 1/2 inches wide and 3/4 inch thick

10 ounces lingue

1 tablespoon finely chopped fresh parsley leaves

Dusting of cayenne pepper

———

1. Prepare a hot charcoal fire or preheat a gas grill 20 minutes on high.

2. In a large skillet, heat the olive oil over medium-high heat and cook the onion and garlic until translucent, 3 to 4 minutes, stirring frequently so the garlic doesn't burn. Add the artichoke hearts and wine, cooking until the wine evaporates to about 1 teaspoon. Pour in the fish broth and add the rosemary sprig, and cook 6 to 7 minutes. Add the oysters and cook until their edges curl up, about 5 minutes. Remove and discard the rosemary sprig. Season with salt and pepper. Remove from the burner and keep warm.

3. Lightly oil, salt, and pepper the salmon and lay on the grill without pushing it around. Leave the salmon undisturbed for 4 to 5 minutes, then turn carefully with a long-handled spatula and grill another 4 to 5 minutes without moving.

4. Meanwhile, bring a large pot of abundantly salted water to a rolling boil and add the pasta. Drain when al dente. Toss the lingue with the sauce in the skillet, lay the grilled salmon on top, sprinkle with parsley and cayenne pepper, and serve.

Grilled Tuna with Salsa Verde

Grilling a round of tuna cut from the tail end is quite nice and an easy way to feed four people. In Italy the same might be done with albacore, bonito, or little tuna (*tunnina*). A good fishmonger should be able to cut it for you; otherwise buy four tuna steaks. This dish can be preceded by Tomato, Artichoke, and Montasio Salad with Green Sauce (page 25).

MAKES 4 SERVINGS

———

One 2-pound tuna steak, cut in 1 round slice from the tail end,
$1/2$ to $3/4$ inch thick
Extra-virgin olive oil
Salt and freshly ground black pepper to taste

FOR THE SALSA VERDE
$1/4$ cup very finely chopped fresh parsley leaves
1 large garlic clove, very finely chopped
6 tablespoons extra-virgin olive oil

———

1. Prepare a charcoal fire or preheat a gas grill on high for 20 minutes.

2. Coat the tuna round lightly with olive oil, salt, and pepper. Place on the grill for 4 to 5 minutes, turn and cook for another 5 to 6 minutes.

3. Meanwhile, combine ingredients for the salsa. Transfer tuna to a serving platter and cover with as much of the salsa as you like. Serve immediately.

Grouper with a Chick-pea Flour Crust

This terrific preparation came about accidently when I found myself without wheat flour, of all things, but with a whole bag of chick-pea flour. Chick-pea flour can be found in whole or natural food markets and in many Italian grocery stores. Grouper is *cernia* in Italian and a beautiful fish for a griddle or grill. You could replace it with red snapper.

MAKES 4 SERVINGS

———

2 tablespoons extra-virgin olive oil
4 grouper fillets (2 pounds total)
1/2 cup chick-pea flour
Salt and freshly ground black pepper to taste
Lemon wedges for garnish

———

1. Heat the olive oil on a large cast-iron griddle over medium-high heat.

2. Meanwhile, dredge the fish in the chick-pea flour seasoned with salt and pepper. Tap off any excess flour and place the fish on the griddle for 7 to 8 minutes without moving them. Flip once and cook another 7 to 8 minutes. Serve with a wedge of lemon.

Batter-Fried Cheap Fish

*O*ne day at a high-quality fish market I was aghast at the prices I was paying. Swordfish was $14 a pound, tuna $15, salmon $11, even cod was $9. This was crazy. There was also a fish called ocean pout for $2.99 a pound. I remembered having heard of it, but couldn't quite place what it was. But I figured, all these fish came from the same ocean, they're all equally fresh, so how bad could ocean pout be? Little did I realize that family and friends would be exclaiming how good this fish, also called ling, was. The texture is vaguely like that of lobster tails, with a taste a little sweeter than monkfish.

MAKES 4 SERVINGS

———

6 cups olive oil or vegetable oil for frying
1 large egg
1/2 cup all-purpose flour
1/2 cup milk
1 tablespoon water
1 teaspoon ground cumin (optional)
1 teaspoon salt
Freshly ground black pepper to taste
1 1/2 pounds ocean pout (ling) or monkfish, cut into 2-inch pieces

———

1. Preheat the frying oil in a deep fryer to 375°F or in an 8-inch saucepan until almost smoking, about 10 minutes.

2. Beat the egg in a bowl, then stir in the flour, milk, water, cumin (if using), salt, and pepper. It should be a thin batter. Dip the fish pieces, a handful at a time, into the batter. Let some of the batter drain off,

then quickly drop them in succession one at a time into the oil. Fry, turning occasionally, until golden brown, 2 to 3 minutes (don't crowd the fryer or pot, you'll have to fry them in several batches). Taste one and adjust the cooking time for the remaining fish to your liking. Salt and serve. Let the frying oil cool, then strain and save.

Grilled Wolffish

The wolffish's diet of sea urchins, clams, and crabs might account for its delicious taste. It's a moist piece of firm-fleshed fish steak that is great on the grill. Wolffish is now called ocean catfish by those clever marketing people.

MAKES 4 TO 6 SERVINGS

―――――

6 wolffish steaks (2 pounds total)
Extra-virgin olive oil
Salt and freshly ground black pepper to taste
1/2 cup dry bread crumbs
1 teaspoon dried oregano
Lemon wedges for garnish

―――――

1. Prepare a charcoal fire or preheat a gas grill on high for 20 minutes.

2. Coat the fish steaks with olive oil and season with salt and pepper. Mix the bread crumbs with the oregano on a plate and dredge the fish steaks in the bread crumbs so all sides are coated.

3. Drizzle a little olive oil on the side of the fish that will touch the grill first. Drizzle some oil on the top side. Place the fish on the grill until golden and crusty, 6 to 8 minutes. Turn and grill another 6 to 8 minutes. Serve with lemon wedges.

Panfried Ocean Pout with Chives

*O*cean pout's firm flesh is ideal for searing in a pan, but you can also replace it with monkfish, freshwater catfish, or mahimahi (dolphinfish). This recipe cooks very fast, so stay close to the pan. Serve with Panfried Yellow Peppers and Mushrooms (page 241) or linguine doused with a smidgen of olive oil.

MAKES 4 SERVINGS

2 tablespoons extra-virgin olive oil
1 garlic clove, crushed
1¹/₂ pounds ocean pout (ling) fillets, cut into 8 pieces
Salt and freshly ground black pepper to taste
3 tablespoons chopped fresh chives

1. Heat the olive oil with the garlic clove in a large skillet over very high heat. Remove and discard the garlic before it begins to turn light brown.

2. When the oil is almost smoking, add the fish carefully to the pan and cook for 1 minute without touching or turning. Season with salt and pepper. Turn to the other side with a spatula and cook for 1 minute.

3. Remove to a serving platter and sprinkle with the chives. Correct the seasonings and serve immediately.

Golden-Crusted Monkfish with Gremolada

I love firm-fleshed fish. Monkfish was completely unknown to Americans twenty years ago, but now is widely available. Both monkfish and the less well known ocean pout (ling) give up narrow fillets perfect for a variety of preparations. This simple recipe can be accompanied by a roasted red bell pepper per person. *Gremolada* is a condiment used in Milan with ossobuco alla Milanese (stewed veal shank), but it's a fine accompaniment to fish, too.

MAKES 4 SERVINGS

1/2 cup tightly packed fresh parsley leaves
6 salted anchovy fillets, rinsed and patted dry
One 1-inch square lemon zest, with no white pith attached
1 cup extra-virgin or virgin olive oil
1 garlic clove, crushed
1 1/2 pounds monkfish or other fish fillets, cut into 2-inch pieces
All-purpose flour for dredging
2 large eggs, beaten
Dry bread crumbs for dredging
Salt and freshly ground black pepper to taste

---

1. Chop the parsley, anchovies, and lemon zest together very finely. Set aside.

2. Heat the olive oil with the garlic clove in a medium-size pan over medium-high heat. Remove and discard the garlic just as it begins to turn light brown.

3. Meanwhile, dredge the fish in the flour, tapping off any excess. Dip in the eggs, and then dredge in the bread crumbs. Fry the fish until a nice golden brown, about 2 minutes per side. Transfer to a serving platter or individual plates, season with salt and pepper, sprinkle with the anchovy mixture, and serve.

Stuffed Squid

Summertime. That's the time for *calamari ripieni,* or stuffed squid. I grill it with olive oil until glistening gold to remind me of a wonderful summer day lunching al fresco in a Sardinian *trattoria* some years ago. This recipe works best with small squid. If the squid you buy is not already cleaned, it takes about 10 minutes to do so (page 164).

Serve this preceded by or on top of Spaghetti with Anchovies, Herbs, and Spices (page 128), with rice, or the variation below.

MAKES 4 SERVINGS

———

1¹/₂ pounds cleaned small squid with their tentacles (about 24 squid)
Juice of ¹/₂ lemon
4 garlic cloves, very finely chopped
¹/₄ cup finely chopped fresh parsley leaves
8 salted anchovy fillets, rinsed, patted dry, and chopped
¹/₂ cup dry bread crumbs
Salt and freshly ground black pepper to taste
2 tablespoons extra-virgin olive oil

———

1. Cut the tentacles off below the eyes and place them in lightly salted boiling water with the lemon juice for 4 minutes. Drain and chop, then mix with the garlic, parsley, anchovies, and bread crumbs and season with salt and pepper.

2. Rinse the squid bodies and dry them on paper towels. Stuff the squids with the bread crumb mixture using a narrow spoon, such as a baby spoon, and close with a toothpick.

3. Place the squid in a large skillet with 2 tablespoons olive oil. Turn the heat to medium-low and cook until the squid are golden brown on both sides, about 40 minutes.

VARIATION: Use 4 tablespoons of olive oil instead of 2 to sauté the squid. Bring a large pot of abundantly salted water to a rolling boil and add ¾ pound vermicelli. Drain when all dente. Remove the squid from the skillet, add the vermicelli to the skillet, sprinkle with 2 tablespoons finely chopped fresh parsley leaves and 2 finely chopped garlic cloves, toss well, transfer to a serving bowl or platter, and top with the reserved squid.

A magical spice, powerful
and expensive, used in
minuscule portions—never
more than a pinch—espe-
cially in Sicilian cuisine. The
threads are more versatile
than powdered saffron.
Saffron is always colored
orange-maroon, never deep
red, which is safflower, sometimes sold to the unknowing
as saffron. If you ever come
across inexpensive saffron,
rest assured it's not saffron. A
so-called pinch of saffron is
about 35 threads, or pistils.
It's best to crumble it in a
mortar with a pestle and then
rinse out the residue with a
few tablespoons of water.
Store in a dark, cool place.

᠎

Sicilian-Style Seafood Stew in Delicious Sauce

One look at the ingredient list and I imagine you've turned the page. Don't: this recipe is just one thing added after another and will take about 40 minutes to prepare and cook. Much of the prep work can be combined. You can chop the garlic, celery, and onion together. You can mix the anchovies, capers, raisins, pine nuts, olives, fennel, and oregano and keep it in the refrigerator until needed. However you choose to do it, you will be rewarded with a heavenly stew. Incidentally, the name is not completely made up: a Sicilian fish soup is known as *ghiotta*, a word that can also mean "delicious."

MAKES 4 TO 6 SERVINGS

———

Pinch of saffron threads
1/4 cup hot water
1 tablespoon sugar
1/4 cup white wine vinegar
2 tablespoons dry white wine
1 tablespoon fresh oregano leaves (optional)
1/2 cup extra-virgin olive oil
2 garlic cloves, chopped
1 small onion, chopped
1 celery stalk, chopped
2 pounds ripe plum tomatoes, peeled, seeded, and chopped
4 salted anchovy fillets, rinsed, patted dry, and chopped
1 1/2 tablespoons capers, rinsed
1 tablespoon golden raisins
1 tablespoon pine nuts
5 large green olives, pitted and chopped

¹/₄ teaspoon fennel seeds
4¹/₂ teaspoons dried oregano
¹/₂ pound sea scallops
¹/₂ pound swordfish steak, cut into the same size pieces as
the scallops
Salt and freshly ground black pepper to taste
4 ounces cooked lobster meat
3 ounces cooked crabmeat, picked over for shells and cartilage
10 ounces cooked medium-size shrimp

———

1. Crumble the saffron in a bowl or mortar and add the hot water, letting the spice steep until needed. Dissolve the sugar in the vinegar and wine, add the fresh oregano, and set aside.

2. In a large, deep casserole, heat the olive oil over medium-high heat and cook the garlic, onion, and celery until translucent, about 4 minutes, stirring often so the garlic doesn't burn. Turn the heat to high, add the tomatoes, and cook until some of the juices have evaporated, about 6 minutes, stirring frequently. Pour in the reserved saffron water and stir, then add the anchovies, capers, raisins, pine nuts, olives, fennel seeds, and dried oregano. Stir again to mix well, cover, and cook for 2 minutes. Add the scallops and swordfish, cover, and cook over medium-high heat for 2 minutes. Season with salt and pepper.

3. Add the sugar-and-vinegar mixture to the sauce and cook, uncovered, for 2 minutes. Taste the sauce and correct for salt, pepper, and oregano. Taste a piece of swordfish; it should be almost done. Add some boiling water if the broth is too thick; it should be a little soupy. Add the lobster, crab, and shrimp and cook for 1 minute. Serve with crostini, or slices of Italian bread fried in garlic-flavored olive oil.

CHAPTER TEN

Vegetables
and Side Dishes

As any family cook knows, getting kids to eat vegetables can be an exercise in cajoling and worry. Long ago I realized that this is a peculiarly American phenomenon. I never met an Italian mom who said she couldn't get the kids to eat vegetables. And I realized why. Italian vegetable cookery is so flavorful that vegetables often become the center of the meal. This chapter has such a short taste of the huge range of Italian vegetable recipes, but I hope you get the idea. In the end, American kids aren't eating vegetables because we American cooks don't put enough effort into cooking them. Here's a sampling of how an Italian family cook would approach the problem and maybe your kids will come to actually ask for Spinaci con Aglio e Olio (page 234) or Batter-Fried Broccoli (page 247). Now that's satisfaction!

There are two basic varieties of spinach available on the market. Savoy spinach is curly leafed, with dark green leaves. This is the most common spinach and the one usually sold in 10-ounce bags.

The other type of spinach is usually sold loose. It is called flat-leafed or Italian spinach, and has smooth, oval-shaped leaves and reddish roots. It is easier to prepare for cooking because the stems are not as thick and the leaves do not curl around the stem. Spinach will keep well three to four days after purchase. The heavy stems should be removed before using and the leaves washed well to remove any dirt or grit. Keep spinach in the refrigerator crisper drawer.

❧

Spinaci con Aglio e Olio

Spinach with garlic and olive oil is the vegetable preparation I make more than any other, partly because of its simplicity but also because the taste is consistently attractive no matter how you accompany the spinach.

MAKES 4 SERVINGS

————

*20 ounces fresh spinach, trimmed of tough stems and
thoroughly washed*
2 to 4 tablespoons extra-virgin olive oil
3 large garlic cloves, finely chopped
Salt and freshly ground black pepper to taste
Juice of 1/2 lemon (optional)

————

1. Place the spinach in a large saucepan with only the water adhering to it from its last rinsing. Cover, turn the heat to medium-high, and cook until the spinach wilts, 4 to 5 minutes, tossing occasionally. Drain very well in a colander or strainer, pressing out the excess water with the back of a wooden spoon.

2. Put the spinach, olive oil, garlic, salt, and pepper in a large skillet and turn the heat to medium-high. As soon as the spinach begins to sizzle, cook for 3 minutes, stirring frequently so the garlic doesn't burn. Transfer to a serving platter and drizzle with the lemon juice, if desired. Serve warm or at room temperature.

Spinach and Fresh Ricotta Gratinate

A golden crust is lovely on this green-and-white side dish. Try it with Broiled Shark with Pesto Trapanese (page 216). You could broil both at the same time for a quick dinner.

MAKES 4 SERVINGS

———

20 ounces fresh spinach, trimmed of tough stems and
thoroughly washed
3 tablespoons extra-virgin olive oil
6 ounces ricotta cheese, preferably fresh
2 garlic cloves (optional), finely chopped
Salt and freshly ground black pepper to taste
¼ cup fresh bread crumbs
2 tablespoons unsalted butter

———

1. Put the spinach in a large saucepan with only the water adhering to it from its last rinsing. Cover the pot and heat over high heat until the spinach wilts, 4 to 5 minutes, tossing occasionally. Drain well, pressing the excess liquid out with the back of a wooden spoon.

2. Preheat the broiler. Lightly oil a small baking casserole or pan with 1 tablespoon of the olive oil and spread the spinach around. Spread the ricotta over the spinach, sprinkle the garlic around, if using, drizzle 1 tablespoon of the olive oil over the top, and season with salt and pepper. Sprinkle the bread crumbs over it all and dot with the butter and remaining tablespoon olive oil. Place under the broiler until the bread crumbs are golden, about 12 minutes, and serve.

Drowned Mustard Greens

This Sicilian-inspired recipe was originally for broccoli but works spectacularly with mustard greens, which Italians don't eat. The Sicilians call this kind of dish *affucati,* or "drowned," because it's smothered in wine. It's terrific as a room temperature appetizer the next day, too.

MAKES 4 SERVINGS

———

¹/4 cup extra-virgin olive oil
1 medium onion, coarsely chopped
4 garlic cloves, finely chopped
4 salted anchovy fillets, rinsed and patted dry
1 pound mustard greens, trimmed of tough stems, thoroughly washed,
and shredded
³/4 cup dry red wine
8 imported black olives, pitted and chopped
Salt and freshly ground black pepper to taste
3 tablespoons freshly grated Parmesan cheese

———

1. In a medium-size casserole or skillet, heat the olive oil over medium-high heat and cook the onion and garlic until they turn color, 3 to 4 minutes, stirring constantly so the garlic doesn't burn. Add the anchovies; once they have melted, add the shredded mustard greens, cover, and cook until they wilt, about 5 minutes.

2. Pour the wine into the sauce along with the olives and season with salt and pepper. Cover again, reduce the heat to medium, and cook for 15 minutes and then taste to see if that's the way you like it.

Transfer to a serving platter with a slotted ladle, sprinkle on the cheese, and serve.

NOTE: If serving the next day as a room temperature antipasto, let the Parmesan cheese melt and then drizzle some olive oil over it to serve.

Dandelion

This is a recipe my grandfather would make for himself. He was Italian, so, as in Italy, he called it "dandelion." The bitter taste of dandelion, which I love on its own, is a natural accompaniment to a rich dish.

MAKES 2 SERVINGS

———

2 tablespoons extra-virgin olive oil
2 tablespoons unsalted butter
2 garlic cloves, finely chopped
1 bunch dandelions (about 3/4 pound), thoroughly washed and shredded
Salt and freshly ground black pepper to taste

———

1. Heat the olive oil and butter together in a large skillet over medium-high heat; when the butter melts, add the garlic and dandelions.

2. Cook until the dandelions wilt and the water from the leaves evaporates, about 10 minutes, stirring occasionally. Season with salt and pepper and serve.

DANDELION

My mother tells the story of how her father, Raphael De Yeso, who was from a small village in southern Italy, would take her to Pelham Bay from their apartment in Manhattan to pick wild dandelions in the spring.

The common lawn dandelion is a delicious green, but it must be picked, root and all, when the leaves are young and before any flower or bud appears. Be careful that pesticide has not been sprayed on the lawn and never pick dandelions near roadways because of automobile exhaust.

This bitter green is used in salads or cooked with olive oil and prosciutto. The dandelions sold in the market are cultivated, making for longer, more tender leaves.

Swiss Chard with
Mascarpone-Gorgonzola Gratinate

Swiss chard is a pretty rugged leafy green vegetable, and for that reason I believe it can handle a strong cheese like Gorgonzola and a gratin top. Save the white central ribs of each leaf to make Swiss Chard Stalk Soup (page 33).

MAKES 2 TO 4 SERVINGS

1½ pounds Swiss chard, thoroughly washed and stems and thick central ribs removed, leaving leaves only
¼ cup mascarpone cheese
3 tablespoons Gorgonzola cheese
2 tablespoons freshly grated Parmesan cheese
2 tablespoons fresh bread crumbs

---

1. Preheat the oven to 450°F.

2. Put the Swiss chard in a pot with only the water adhering to it from its last rinsing. Cover the pot, turn the heat to high, and cook until it wilts, about 4 minutes. Turn with a wooden spoon and continue cooking, uncovered, until the water is nearly evaporated, another 4 to 5 minutes. Drain well and chop.

3. Blend the mascarpone, Gorgonzola, and Parmesan cheeses together in a small bowl. Stir in the Swiss chard. Spoon the chard into a small baking pan. Sprinkle with the bread crumbs and place in the oven until golden brown, 8 to 10 minutes.

Zucchini with Pecorino

This delicious preparation can be served hot or at room temperature, as an antipasto or a side dish.

MAKES 2 TO 4 SERVINGS

————

1 pound baby zucchini, peeled and sliced
3 tablespoons extra-virgin olive oil
1 garlic clove, crushed
Salt and freshly ground black pepper to taste
Ground red chili or cayenne pepper to taste
1 to 2 tablespoons freshly grated Pecorino cheese

————

1. Leave the sliced zucchini in a strainer in the sink to leach some of its juice for 30 minutes. Pat dry with paper towels.

2. Heat 2 tablespoons of the olive oil in a medium-size skillet with the garlic over medium-high heat. Before the garlic begins to turn light brown, remove and discard. Cook the zucchini until golden brown, tossing or stirring often, 10 to 12 minutes. Season with salt, black pepper, and a dusting of red pepper.

3. Transfer to a serving platter, drizzle with the remaining tablespoon olive oil, and sprinkle on the cheese. Serve immediately or at room temperature.

Green Beans and Mushroom Contorno

A *contorno* is a side dish eaten with a main course. This *contorno* is best served at room temperature and goes great with chicken. Wipe the mushrooms clean with a paper towel; do not wash them.

MAKES 4 SERVINGS

3/4 pound green beans, trimmed
1/4 cup extra-virgin olive oil
3/4 pound mushrooms, sliced
1 garlic clove, finely chopped
2 tablespoons finely chopped fresh parsley leaves
4 salted anchovy fillets, rinsed and patted dry
Pinch of red pepper flakes
Salt and freshly ground black pepper to taste
1/4 cup dry Marsala wine

1. Bring a saucepan of lightly salted water to a boil and blanch the green beans for 4 minutes. Drain, rinse in cold water, and set aside.

2. Heat the olive oil in a medium-size skillet over medium-high heat. Add the mushrooms, garlic, parsley, anchovies, and red pepper, season with salt and pepper, and cook until the mushrooms are brown, about 10 minutes, stirring frequently. Add the green beans and wine, and continue cooking until all the liquid has evaporated, about 5 minutes. Transfer to a serving platter and serve at room temperature.

Panfried Yellow Peppers and Mushrooms

Here's a beautiful accompaniment to grilled meats or panfried fish that you can finish in 15 minutes. Use any kind of mushroom, although portobellos, for instance, will provide an earthier taste.

MAKES 4 SERVINGS

---

2 tablespoons extra-virgin olive oil
4 garlic cloves, crushed
2 yellow bell peppers, seeded and thinly sliced
1 pound portobello mushrooms, cleaned and sliced
Salt and freshly ground black pepper to taste
2 tablespoons finely chopped fresh parsley leaves

---

1. Heat the olive oil in a large skillet over high heat. Add the garlic, yellow peppers, and mushrooms, season with salt and pepper, and cook until the peppers are soft and mushrooms brown, 12 to 14 minutes, stirring frequently. Whenever the liquid evaporates, add 2 tablespoons water, and keep adding until the final minute of cooking. The skillet should be dry when you finish cooking. Sprinkle the parsley on top, toss, and transfer to a serving platter. Serve immediately.

Asparagus and Portobello Mushrooms

Little spears of fresh asparagus, bright green and delectable, are contrasted with the earthy mushrooms.

MAKES 4 SERVINGS

———

2 tablespoons extra-virgin olive oil
1 pound asparagus, bottoms trimmed and cut into 1^1/$_2$-inch lengths
1 pound portobello mushrooms, cleaned and sliced
2 garlic cloves, finely chopped
Salt and freshly ground black pepper to taste
1^1/$_2$ cups dry red wine or water, or more as needed
Freshly grated ricotta salata

———

1. Heat the olive oil in a large skillet over medium-high heat. Add the asparagus, mushrooms, and garlic, and cook until the mushrooms turn a little brown, about 3 minutes, stirring often. Season with salt and pepper. Pour in 1 cup of the wine, turn the heat to high, and cook for 20 minutes, adding lesser and lesser amounts of the wine, to keep the pan moist. When the asparagus are almost cooked, put no more liquid in the pan and leave it to cook until all the liquid has evaporated and they are tender. Transfer to a serving platter and serve immediately with grated ricotta salata.

Fennel Gratinate

Although fennel is a favorite Italian vegetable, many Americans shy away from it because of its distinct anise taste. But that's what makes it so interesting! Try this recipe, which treats fennel in a different manner, and accompany it with Costalette alla Milanese (page 194) for a surprising change.

MAKES 4 SERVINGS

———

3 medium-size fennel bulbs (1¹/₂ to 1³/₄ pounds)
2 tablespoons unsalted butter
1 tablespoon extra-virgin olive oil
1 garlic clove, crushed
Salt and freshly ground black pepper to taste
2 tablespoons water
6 to 8 tablespoons fresh bread crumbs

———

1. Preheat the oven to 450°F.

2. Bring a pot of lightly salted water to a boil. Blanch the whole fennel bulbs for 6 to 7 minutes. Drain and slice.

3. Melt 1 tablespoon of the butter with the olive oil and garlic in a large skillet over high heat. Once the butter begins to bubble, add the fennel, season with salt and pepper, and cook until brown on the edges, about 6 minutes, stirring or shaking the skillet vigorously.

4. Transfer to a buttered baking pan. Add the water to the skillet, scrape the browned bits off the bottom, and pour over the fennel. Sprinkle the bread crumbs on top, dot with slivers of the remaining tablespoon of butter, and bake until the top is golden, 12 to 15 minutes.

Summertime Broccoli

This is a way of making broccoli when the temperature skyrockets and you don't feel like eating hot, steaming food. This recipe is really very simple—just a platter of bright green broccoli with a little seasoning served at room temperature.

MAKES 4 SERVINGS

———

1½ pounds broccoli, trimmed of heavy stems
Extra-virgin olive oil
Freshly squeezed lemon juice
Salt and freshly ground black pepper to taste

———

1. Blanch the broccoli by plunging it into vigorously boiling water for 3 minutes. Drain in a strainer or colander and plunge into ice water or run under cold tap water to stop the cooking.

2. Once the broccoli is cool, you can steam or boil it whole until easily pierced with a skewer but still bright green, about 8 minutes or less. Drain well, patting dry with paper towels if necessary.

3. Break into florets on a serving platter, drizzle with olive oil and lemon juice, and season with salt and pepper. Serve at room temperature or slightly warm.

Broccoli in Tomato Sauce

This is the kind of preparation I like to make in the summer and serve with grilled foods. The broccoli is simmered with the tomatoes and then served at room temperature.

MAKES 4 SERVINGS

———

2 tablespoons extra-virgin olive oil
1 small onion, chopped
2 garlic cloves, finely chopped
1 pound ripe tomatoes, peeled, seeded, and chopped
½ cup dry white wine
½ cup water
Salt and freshly ground black pepper to taste
1 pound broccoli, broken into small florets

———

1. Heat the olive oil in a large skillet or casserole over medium-high heat and cook the onion and garlic until translucent, about 4 minutes, stirring frequently so the garlic doesn't burn.

2. Add the tomatoes, wine, and water; season with salt and pepper; and cook another 2 minutes, stirring. Add the broccoli, reduce the heat to medium-low, stir, and cook until the broccoli is tender, about 30 minutes. Moisten with water if the sauce dries out.

Broccoli and Roasted Red Bell Pepper

Good and good for you. That was a phrase I often heard from my mom when I was growing up. She never quite made it this way, but this Italian family-style *contorno* of bright green broccoli and brilliant red bell pepper is a delight to look at, delicious to eat, and good for you.

MAKES 4 SERVINGS

———

1¹/₂ pounds broccoli, broken into florets and heavy stems sliced
1 roasted red bell pepper, jarred or freshly made, sliced into strips
¹/₃ cup extra-virgin olive oil
2 garlic cloves, very finely chopped
2 tablespoons freshly squeezed lemon juice

———

1. In a covered medium-size saucepan over boiling water, steam the broccoli until it is slightly resistant to the piercing of a skewer, about 10 minutes.

2. Drain a bit and transfer to a mixing bowl. Toss with the remaining ingredients and arrange on a serving platter.

Batter-Fried Broccoli

I love vegetables, especially preparations that are Italian or Mediterranean in any way. My kids, on the other hand, although they will actually eat some vegetables, never have more than the minuscule portions I put on their plate, except for Spinaci con Aglio e Olio (page 234) and this recipe, the only version of broccoli they'll ask for seconds and thirds. I usually serve this with fried fish.

MAKES 4 SERVINGS

———

1 cup all-purpose flour
Salt and freshly ground black pepper to taste
1 tablespoon olive oil
1 cup beer (lager)
2 large egg whites
1 pound broccoli, broken into florets
6 cups olive oil or vegetable oil

———

1. Sift the flour, salt, and pepper into a mixing bowl. Make a well in the center and add oil and beer. Gradually mix with the flour until smooth; do not overmix. Let stand for 1 hour. Beat the egg whites in a medium-size bowl until stiff peaks form. Fold into batter.

2. Heat the frying oil in a deep fryer to 375°F or in an 8-inch saucepan over medium-high heat until almost smoking, about 10 minutes.

3. Dip the broccoli in the batter, let some of the batter drip off, and deep-fry in the hot oil until golden, about 2 minutes, turning if necessary. Make sure not to crowd the fryer or pan; otherwise, the food will be greasy. Drain on paper towels, salt lightly, and keep warm while you finish cooking. Serve immediately.

Broccoliflower with Bagna Cauda

Broccoliflower is a light green cauliflower. They love this vegetable in Sicily, calling it *vrucculu*. This recipe is the perfect accompaniment to Chicken Saltimbocca (page 207).

MAKES 4 SERVINGS

————

1½ pounds broccoliflower (or a combination of half cauliflower and half broccoli)
6 tablespoons extra-virgin olive oil
2 garlic cloves, crushed
2 dried red chili peppers, crumbled (about ½ teaspoon)
2 salted anchovy fillets, rinsed, patted dry, and chopped

————

1. Bring a couple of cups of water to a boil in a steamer over high heat. Reduce the heat to medium and put the whole broccoliflower in the steamer and steam until easily penetrated by a skewer, about 10 minutes.

2. Meanwhile, heat the olive oil, garlic, chili peppers, and anchovies in a small saucepan. Once the broccoliflower is done, separate into florets, pour the sauce over, and serve.

Broiled Potato and Cheese Patties

This recipe is so delicious that I will go ahead and make mashed potatoes simply to have this dish. The taste is great, reminiscent of *mozzarella in carroza*, a bread or bread crumb-coated piece of cheese fried in olive oil until golden and crispy. Remember: the anchovies are essential, so don't leave them out.

MAKES 4 SERVINGS

———

1/2 cup virgin olive oil
1 1/2 cups leftover mashed potatoes
1 large egg, beaten
Dry bread crumbs for dredging
Salt and freshly ground black pepper to taste
6 ounces fresh mozzarella cheese, sliced
1/2 cup canned tomato puree
8 salted anchovy fillets, rinsed and patted dry

———

1. Preheat the broiler.

2. Heat the olive oil in a large skillet over medium-high heat until the oil is nearly smoking.

3. Form the leftover mashed potatoes into 8 patties with wet hands, to prevent sticking. Dip in the beaten egg and then dredge in the bread crumbs on all sides. Dip in the egg again and dredge again in the bread crumbs.

continued

4. Cook the potato patties in the skillet on both sides until golden brown. Remove and place in a lightly oiled baking pan. Salt and pepper lightly. Layer the mozzarella slices on top and cover with the tomato puree. Broil until the cheese melts. Layer the anchovy fillets on top and serve.

Griddled Potato Crispelle
with Salmon Caviar and Mascarpone

Very easy to prepare. Very versatile. These crispelle take about 15 minutes and can be served as quite an elegant antipasto. Alternatively you can pull out a cast-iron griddle and make them at the same time you make Grouper with a Chick-pea Flour Crust (page 221). Maybe you can even cook them for breakfast—I did once and they were fantastic.

MAKES 4 SERVINGS

———

2 tablespoons extra-virgin olive oil
2 large potatoes (about 1 1/2 pounds)
3 tablespoons finely chopped onion
2 garlic cloves, finely chopped
Salt and freshly ground black pepper to taste
2 tablespoons whipped butter
2 to 3 ounces salmon caviar
2 ounces mascarpone cheese

———

1. Spread the olive oil on a cast-iron griddle and heat over medium-high heat until it begins to smoke.

2. Meanwhile, peel the potatoes and grate them quickly into a bowl. Mix with the onion and garlic and season liberally with salt and pepper. Divide the potato mixture in half and place each half over the portion of the griddle that rests on a burner. Flatten them into crepes (that is, crispelle) with a spatula until they are about 1/8 inch thick on the bottom. Cook until golden brown, about 7 to 8 minutes. Flip over and cook for another 7 to 8 minutes.

3. Remove from the heat and spread the butter over the hot crispelle. Then spread the salmon caviar and mascarpone over them. Fold in half, cut in half, and serve immediately.

Sorrel is related to rhubarb,
but it is usually used as a
salad green or in soups.
Sorrel has a slightly bitter,
lemonlike taste. It can be
replaced with watercress or
arugula, although both have
very different flavors.

∾

Tomato with Basil and Sorrel

This is a very simple dish. The natural sweetness of ripe tomatoes mingles with the aromatic basil and ever so slightly bitter sorrel for a delightful preparation that partners well with grilled meat.

MAKES 4 SERVINGS

————

3 large, very ripe tomatoes (about 1½ pounds total), sliced
12 large fresh sorrel leaves
6 fresh basil leaves, ripped
Extra-virgin olive oil for drizzling
Salt and freshly ground black pepper to taste

————

1. Arrange the tomatoes attractively on a serving platter. Ring the tomatoes with the sorrel leaves and sprinkle the basil on top.

2. Drizzle with olive oil and season with salt and pepper.

VARIATION: Replace the basil with fresh tarragon and sprinkle with diced imported fresh water buffalo mozzarella.

Four Onions with Lentils

Leftover lentils can be sparked up with four members of the onion family for a very flavorful side dish. If you don't happen to have left-over lentils, boil ¾ cup brown lentils in water or chicken broth for about 15 minutes to 1 hour, depending on how old they are. Keep tasting. (It is not necessary to presoak lentils.)

MAKES 2 TO 4 SERVINGS

———

½ small onion, peeled
1 large garlic clove, peeled
3 scallions, white parts with a little of the green
3 shallots, peeled
Leaves from 3 sprigs fresh parsley
Leaves from 1 sprig fresh coriander (cilantro)
6 tablespoons extra-virgin olive oil
1 cup leftover cooked lentils
Salt and freshly ground black pepper to taste

———

1. Chop the onion, garlic, scallions, shallots, parsley, and coriander together very finely.

2. Heat the olive oil in a medium-size skillet over medium-high heat and cook the onion mixture until softened, about 8 minutes, stirring frequently. Add the lentils, season with salt and pepper, cook until they are heated through, about 5 minutes, and serve.

Chick-peas with Pancetta and Ricotta Sauce

This preparation can easily be served as a main course, attractive to the cook because it takes only about 10 minutes to make. If you serve it as a side dish, pair it with a simple chicken dish such as Chicken and Spinach (page 201).

MAKES 4 SERVINGS

———

³/₄ cup ricotta cheese
6 tablespoons water
¹/₃ pound pancetta, cut into small dice
3 tablespoons extra-virgin olive oil
4 cups canned cooked chick-peas, drained
Salt and freshly ground black pepper to taste
2 to 3 tablespoons finely chopped fresh mint leaves
2 to 3 tablespoons freshly grated Pecorino cheese

———

1. Stir the ricotta and water together in a small bowl and set aside.

2. Put the pancetta in a large skillet with the olive oil and heat over medium-high heat. Once the pancetta begins to turn crispy, add the chick-peas and shake the pan so the moisture on the chick-peas will lift up the crust on the bottom of the pan. Shake or stir until the chick-peas are heated through, 2 to 3 minutes. Season with salt and pepper.

3. Stir the ricotta into the chick-peas off the heat until blended. Reduce the heat to low, then return the saucepan to the heat and cook until heated through again, about 2 minutes more. Add the mint, stir, sprinkle with the Pecorino, and serve.

Chick-peas and Artichoke Hearts with Red Tuna Sauce

This is as simple and as good as it gets using canned foods, and that's pretty good. This preparation also uses leftover sauce from Fusilli with Red Tuna Sauce (page 139). It's a wonderful side dish and is also a very well-received antipasto.

MAKES 4 SERVINGS

————

One 1-pound 4-ounce can cooked chick-peas, drained
One 14-ounce can artichoke hearts, drained and cut up
$^1/_4$ cup red tuna sauce (page 139)
2 to 3 tablespoons extra-virgin olive oil
Freshly ground black pepper to taste

————

1. Toss all the ingredients together in a large serving bowl.

2. Serve at room temperature.

Roasted Country Bread with Ricotta and Spinach

The next four recipes are delicious preparations substantial enough to serve as vegetable main courses. Myself, I am a vegophile rather than a vegetarian, and I love satisfying dishes like these four on top of roasted country bread. I also prepare this recipe for lunch when I have leftover spinach.

The country bread that is ideal for this dish is the large round loaf, sometimes called Tuscan bread, that can always be found in an Italian grocery market and many local bread bakeries.

MAKES 4 SERVINGS

———

*10 ounces fresh spinach, trimmed of tough stems and
thoroughly washed*
3 tablespoons unsalted butter
6 tablespoons extra-virgin olive oil
1 garlic clove, crushed
Salt and freshly ground black pepper to taste
*4 large slices round Italian (Tuscan) or French country bread, cut from
the center, each slice about 6 by 8 inches and 3/4 inch thick*
1 pound ricotta cheese, preferably fresh

———

1. Preheat the oven to 350°F.

2. Put the spinach in a large saucepan with only the water adhering to it from its last rinsing. Cover the pot and over medium-high heat wilt the spinach, 4 to 5 minutes, tossing occasionally. Drain well,

using the back of a wooden spoon to squeeze out all water. Chop coarsely.

3. In a medium-size skillet, melt the butter with 2 tablespoons of the olive oil and the crushed garlic. Add the spinach and cook for 5 minutes over medium heat. Season with salt and pepper. Set aside and keep warm.

4. Meanwhile, coat the slices of bread with the ricotta cheese. Drizzle 1 tablespoon of the olive oil over each slice and season with salt and pepper. Set on a baking sheet and place in the oven until the oil starts bubbling, about 10 minutes. Remove from the oven and cover each slice with the spinach. Return to the oven for 2 minutes and then serve.

Country Bread with Tomatoes, Olives, and Red Onions

This is another version of the previous recipe. These two preparations can also be served as appetizers on small toast points, but I prefer them as my main course. The best tomatoes for this recipe are the cultivars known as Big Boys.

MAKES 4 SERVINGS

continued

8 large, very ripe tomatoes (about 3¹/₂ pounds), peeled if desired, seeded, and chopped
1¹/₂ cups chopped imported green olives
2 small red onions, chopped
2 ounces sliced soppresatta or other salami cut into strips (optional)
2 tablespoons finely chopped fresh mint leaves
Coarse salt and coarsely ground black pepper to taste
4 large slices round Italian (Tuscan) or French country bread, cut from the center, each slice about 6 by 8 inches and ³/₄ inch thick
¹/₄ to ³/₄ cup extra-virgin olive oil

1. Preheat the oven to 350°F.

2. In a large bowl, mix the tomatoes, olives, onions, soppresatta, and mint and season with salt and pepper.

3. Arrange the bread slices on a baking sheet and place in the oven until the bread is hard on top but not brown, about 5 minutes. Remove and place a slice on each dinner plate. Spoon the tomato mixture equally over each slice of bread and drizzle about 2 to 3 tablespoons olive oil over each. Serve.

VARIATION: Use an equal amount of green and black olives, replace the mint with basil leaves, and dispense with the onions and salami.

Roasted Country Bread with Ripe Tomatoes and Fresh Basil

I once served this simple preparation in the summer as a main course and everyone found it not only delicious but satisfying, not once asking what else was being served. The tomatoes are piled high and the plate looks quite substantial. I like to grow the large tomatoes known as Big Boys, which are perfect for this when picked ripe off the vine.

MAKES 4 SERVINGS

---

8 large, very ripe tomatoes (about 3¹/₂ pounds), peeled if desired, seeded, and chopped
¹/₄ cup finely chopped fresh basil leaves
Coarse salt and coarsely and freshly ground black pepper to taste
4 large slices round Italian (Tuscan) or French country bread, cut from the center, each slice about 6 by 8 inches and ³/₄ inch thick
¹/₄ to ³/₄ cup extra-virgin olive oil

1. Preheat the oven to 350°F.

2. In a large bowl, mix the tomatoes and basil and season with salt and pepper.

3. Arrange the bread slices on a baking sheet and place in the oven until the bread is hard on top but not brown, about 5 minutes. Remove and place a slice on each dinner plate. Spoon the tomato mixture equally over each slice of bread and drizzle about 1 to 3 tablespoons olive oil over each. Serve.

CHAPTER ELEVEN

Desserts

A NECTARINE, AN ORANGE, a peach. That's what an Italian home cook is likely to serve the family after dinner—fruit and only fruit. Perhaps she might set out some store-bought biscotti and serve some espresso, too. The point is that desserts as we know them, luscious rich cakes and so forth, are not eaten after a meal in Italy. Normally these rich desserts are eaten as part of an afternoon coffee, or at any other time.

I encourage you to set out a bowl of mixed fruits for your family after dinner. Continue your conversation while you pick a grape here and there, finish off a succulent apricot, or sink your teeth into a delicious apple. But if you must have dessert, the recipes in this chapter are all (with one exception) fruit-based treats that will satisfy all family members.

Strawberries in Syrup

When strawberries are in season and not expensive, we buy tons and prepare them in this way, keeping the refrigerator full; but they can't stay too long there because they will start to ferment.

———

2 quarts fresh strawberries (about 1¹/₂ pounds), hulled, rinsed, and halved or quartered
5 tablespoons sugar, or more to taste
1 teaspoon freshly squeezed lemon juice (optional)

———

1. Toss the strawberries, sugar and lemon juice, if using, together in a large bowl in the morning. Refrigerate.

2. Serve at supper.

Strawberries and Grapes in Syrup with Mint and Vanilla

This is a very attractive dish, the strawberries bright red and glistening in the sugar syrup, punctuated by delectable green grapes. The mint and vanilla should provide only a hint of their flavor.

MAKES 4 SERVINGS

———

2 quarts fresh strawberries (about 1¹/₂ pounds), hulled, rinsed, and halved or quartered
¹/₂ pound seedless green grapes
¹/₄ cup sugar
1 teaspoon finely chopped fresh mint leaves
¹/₄ teaspoon pure vanilla extract

———

1. Mix the strawberries, grapes, and sugar in a large bowl in the morning and leave in the refrigerator until you come home that evening.

2. Stir in the mint and vanilla, and let rest outside of the refrigerator until served.

Floating Islands in a Raspberry Sea

*V*isually, this dessert is stunning, but it's the taste of the raspberry syrup that sends me into ecstasy.

MAKES 4 SERVINGS

———

FOR THE MERINGUES
4 large egg whites
$1/4$ cup superfine sugar
$1/2$ teaspoon pure vanilla extract

FOR THE RASPBERRY SAUCE
1 cup granulated sugar
$1/2$ cup water
1 pint fresh raspberries (about 10 ounces), rinsed
2 slices lemon
2 tablespoons framboise or kirsch liqueur
8 large fresh mint leaves

———

1. Preheat the oven to 400°F.

2. Whip the egg whites, superfine sugar, and vanilla together with an electric mixer in a medium-size bowl until stiff peaks form.

3. Butter a baking sheet and spoon out the egg white mixture in 8 large dollops onto it. Bake until the tops are golden brown, about 5 minutes.

4. Meanwhile, prepare the raspberry sauce. Cook the granulated sugar and water together in a small saucepan over high heat until the

sugar is very gooey and thick looking, about 230°F on a candy thermometer. Add the raspberries, lemon slices, and liqueur and stir, breaking up the berries, about 1 minute.

5. Pass the mixture through a food mill or strainer. Return to the saucepan or a microwaveable dish and heat slightly over the burner or in a microwave.

6. Pour the heated raspberry sauce onto 4 shallow individual bowls, set 2 meringue islands in the middle, and serve with mint for garnish.

Ripe Peaches in Rose Water Syrup

This is a great way to use up peaches when they are on the verge of being overripe. Rose water is distilled from the flowers. It can be found in supermarkets, but you'll probably need to ask where they keep it. A Middle Eastern market will sell it for much less.

MAKES 4 SERVINGS

————

6 ripe peaches, peeled, pitted, and sliced
1/2 cup sugar
1/4 teaspoon rose water

————

1. Mix the peaches, sugar, and rose water in a large bowl. Leave in the refrigerator until the sugar has dissolved.

2. Stir and serve when ever you want.

Raspberries and Peaches

Raspberries and peaches—probably my two favorite fruits. In this preparation, I simply toss them together. Make sure the peaches are ripe.

MAKES 2 SERVINGS

———

¹/₂ pint fresh raspberries, rinsed
2 ripe peaches, peeled, pitted, and diced
¹/₄ cup sugar
Whipped cream to taste
8 fresh mint leaves

———

1. Toss the raspberries, peaches, and sugar together in a serving bowl.

2. Top with a dollop of whipped cream, scatter the mint leaves around, and serve.

Mango in Lime Syrup

The mango is a tropical fruit that has found its way into Italian cooking. This recipe is adapted from Antonio Carluccio's *A Taste of Italy*, and is a quick way to take advantage of ripe mangoes.

MAKES 4 SERVINGS

———

Zest and juice of 2 limes
¹/₂ cup sugar
2 tablespoons water
2 ripe mangoes, peeled
8 fresh mint leaves

———

1. Slice the lime zest, without any of the white pith, into very, very fine julienned strips. Set aside.

2. Bring the lime juice, sugar, and water to a gentle boil over medium heat in a small nonreactive saucepan, stirring. Once the sugar has dissolved, add the lime strips and simmer for another 3 to 4 minutes. Let cool.

3. Slice the mangoes as close to their flat pits as you can. Slice each half into sections and arrange decoratively on a platter. Pour the lime syrup over the mangoes and garnish with mint leaves.

Vanilla Fritters

Fried dough, a New England favorite, is known in Italy by a number of different names, including *zeppole*. These fritters are an easy delight to whip up.

MAKES 2 TO 3 SERVINGS

1 cup all-purpose flour
2 tablespoons granulated sugar
1/2 teaspoon salt
1 large egg
1/3 cup milk
1/8 teaspoon pure vanilla extract
6 cups vegetable oil
2 tablespoons unsalted butter, melted
Confectioners' sugar for garnish
Ground cinnamon for garnish

1. Mix the flour, granulated sugar, and salt in a medium-size bowl. Beat the egg in a small bowl and stir in the milk and vanilla. Pour this mixture into the flour and combine until a thick, sticky dough forms.

2. Preheat the frying oil in a deep fryer to 375°F or in an 8-inch saucepan until almost smoking, about 10 minutes. Spoon drop egg-size pieces of the dough into the oil, being careful not to crowd the fryer or pan (you'll probably have to cook the dough in 2 or 3 batches). Cook until light brown, 2 to 3 minutes, turning once if necessary. Remove and drain on paper towels. Test the first one to see if

it is cooked. Adjust the cooking time and continue with the rest of the zeppole. Brush on some butter and sprinkle with confectioners' sugar and cinnamon.

Vanilla Meringue with Warm Orange Blossom Honey

This is a quick way to use egg whites you might have leftover from making another preparation. I like to serve these meringues with tea or an after-dinner cordial.

MAKES 4 SERVINGS

———

2 large egg whites
2 tablespoons sugar
1/8 teaspoon pure vanilla extract
1/4 cup warm orange blossom honey

———

1. Preheat the oven to 400°F.

2. Whip together the egg whites, sugar, and vanilla with an electric mixer in a medium-size bowl until stiff peaks form.

3. Butter a baking sheet and spoon out the egg white mixture in 4 large dollops onto it. Bake until streaked golden brown on the ridges of the meringues, about 5 minutes.

4. Transfer to a serving platter, pour the warm honey on top, and serve.

INDEX

artichoke hearts (*continued*)
  penne with chick-peas and
    mint, 58–59
  sauce, chicken scallopine with,
    204–205
  tomato and Montasio salad
    with green sauce, 25
artichokes, 106–107
arugula, 28
  -basil sauce, pennette with
    scallops and, 166–167
  and Boston lettuce salad with
    walnuts, 28
Asiago, 44
  pine nut and red bell pepper
    frittata, 44
asparagus:
  and portobello mushrooms, 242
  tomato and hearts of palm
    panino, 15

B

baby meatballs in green and white
  sauce, 188–189
bagna cauda, broccoliflower with,
  248
basil, 70
  arugula sauce, pennette with
    scallops and, 166–167
  fresh, roasted country bread
    with tomatoes and, 259
  -garlic whipped cream, capellini
    with, 72
  linguine diavolo with olives
    and, 70
  shrimp and celery sauce,
    fettuccine with, 170–171
  tomato sauce, linguine with red
    snapper in, 157–158
  tomato with sorrel and, 252

batter-fried cheap fish, 222–223
bavette:
  con salsa rossa di tonno alla
    diavolo, 141
  with tuna, 140
bay leaf, sirloin tip and onion,
  grilled, 186
beans, baby lima, gemelli with
  chestnuts and, 66–67
beans, fava, tomato, olive and
  mozzarella salad, 26
beans, green:
  and mushroom contorno, 240
  and tuna, linguine with, 138
beans, navy, fagioli con
  gamberetti, 16–17
beet leaves, tuna, and olives,
  orecchiette with, 135–136
beets, 31–32
  really spectacular potluck pasta
    and vegetable salad, 30–31
bell peppers, *see* pepper(s), bell
Bel Paese, 77
bluefish, spaghetti with, 150–151
Boston lettuce and arugula salad
  with walnuts, 28
bread, 152–153
  country, with tomatoes, olives,
    and red onions, 257–258
  roasted country, with ricotta, 9
  roasted country, with ricotta
    and spinach, 256–257
  roasted country, with ripe
    tomatoes and fresh basil, 259
broccoli, 20–21
  baked penne with tomato and
    anchovy sauce, 130
  batter-fried, 247
  green and yellow salad, 22
  really spectacular potluck pasta
    and vegetable salad, 30–31

and roasted red bell pepper, 246
  summertime, 244
  in tomato sauce, 245
  and white onion salad, 20–21
broccoliflower with bagna cauda,
  248
broccoli rabe, 178
  crayfish and portobello mush-
    rooms, risotto of, 178–179
butter, 49
  anchovy and parsley, 3
  anchovy and parsley, linguine
    with, 126

C

Caciocavallo, 10
  fried, 10
capellini:
  with basil-garlic whipped
    cream, 72
  with ground lamb and tomato
    sauce, 110–111
caper(s), 137
  anchovy and mint sauce,
    linguine with, 137
carrot and radicchio salad, 29
cavatelli with creamy cheese
  fondue, 74–75
caviar, salmon, griddled potato
  crispelle with mascarpone
  and, 250–251
celery:
  really spectacular potluck pasta
    and vegetable salad, 30–31
  shrimp and basil sauce,
    fettuccine with, 170–171
  and tomato sauce, penne with,
    56–57
celery heart, penne with
  peperoncini and, 57–58

ground, capellini with tomato
sauce and, 110–111
with mushrooms and onions,
197
and rosemary sauce, penne
with, 111–112
lasagne:
with chicken, spinach, and
portobello mushrooms,
122–123
free-form, with exotic
mushroom sauce, 64–65
free-form, with olive and
pancetta sauce, 87–88
instant, 108–109
lasagnette with pancetta and
white onions, 81
lemon zest, penne rigate with
fennel and, 60
lentil(s):
four onions with, 253
minestrone, easy, 37
lettuce:
Boston, and arugula salad with
walnuts, 28
cigars (involtini di lattuga), 7
and milk soup, cold, 34
lime syrup, mango in, 267
ling (ocean pout):
batter-fried, 222–223
panfried, with chives, 225
lingue, grilled salmon with
artichoke, oyster, and
rosemary sauce on,
218–219
linguine:
with anchovy, caper, and mint
sauce, 137
with anchovy and parsley
butter, 126
with baby zucchini, 61

with clam and squid sauce,
164–165
diavolo with olives and basil, 70
with garlicky fried oysters,
161–162
with garlicky fried soft-shell
clams, 162–163
with grilled pork chops and
oregano flower buds,
118–119
with hake in anchovy sauce,
152–153
with peppery chicken and
tomato sauce, 121
with red snapper in tomato
basil sauce, 157–158
with salmon, 154
with sardines, olives, and green
peppers, 134–135
with swordfish nuggets,
146–147
with tuna and green beans, 138
verde with panfried pork and
red bell peppers, 116–117
verde with pork, pancetta, and
cream sauce, 114–115
liver(s):
chicken, risotto with wine and,
175–176
veal, with scallions and
Marsala, 192
very quick Venetian-style, 193
lobster, Sicilian-style seafood stew
in delicious sauce, 230-231

M

malfadine:
with chicken and ricotta
almond sauce, 119–120
with olives and garlic, 71

mango in lime syrup, 267
marrow, beef, 12
marrow, veal, 12
crostini, 12
Marsala, veal liver with scallions
and, 192
mascarpone, 74
-Gorgonzola gratinate, Swiss
chard with, 238
griddled potato crispelle with
salmon caviar and, 250–251
sauce, fettuccine with, 75
meat, 181–207
see also specific meats
meatballs, baby, in green and
white sauce, 188–189
meringue, vanilla, with warm
orange blossom honey, 269
mezze ziti with pancetta,
prosciutto, pistachios, and
peas, 88–89
milk and lettuce soup, cold, 34
minestrone, easy lentil, 37
mint:
anchovy and caper sauce,
linguine with, 137
penne with chick-peas and,
58–59
and scallion frittata, 41
strawberries and grapes in
syrup with vanilla and, 263
monkfish, golden-crusted, with
gremolada, 226–227
Montasio, tomato and artichoke
salad with green sauce, 25
mozzarella, 108–109
broiled potato and cheese
patties, 249–250
instant lasagne, 108–109
sausage and tomato sauce
frittata, 47

mozzarella (*continued*)
tomato, fava, and olive salad, 26
mushroom(s), 64–65
frittata, 42
and green beans contorno, 240
and onions, lamb with, 197
portobello, chicken and spinach, lasagne with, 122–123
portobello, crayfish and broccoli rabe, risotto of, 178–179
sauce, exotic, free-form lasagne with, 64–65
shiitake, grilled veal chops and spaghettini with yellow squash and, 190–191
and yellow peppers, panfried, 241
mustard greens, drowned, 236–237

O

ocean catfish, grilled, 224
ocean pout (ling):
batter-fried, 222–223
panfried, with chives, 225
olive(s), 6
beet leaves and tuna, orecchiette with, 135–136
black, and ricotta salata in olive oil, 6
linguine diavolo with basil and, 70
malfadine with garlic and, 71
and pancetta sauce, free-form lasagne with, 87–88
perciatelli with sausages and, 96–97

sardines and green peppers, linguine with, 134–135
sun salad, 24
tomato, fava, and mozzarella salad, 26
tomatoes and red onions, country bread with, 257–258
olive oil, 8
red pepper, 92
ricotta salata and black olives in, 6
spinaci con aglio e olio, 234
onion(s):
chicken with three, 206
four, with lentils, 253
golden, pork chops and, 196
grilled sirloin tip, bay leaf and, 186
and mushrooms, lamb with, 197
red, tomatoes and olives, country bread with, 257–258
white, and broccoli salad, 20–21
white, lasagnette with pancetta and, 81
orange and swordfish, grilled skewers of, 214–215
orange blossom honey, warm, vanilla meringue with, 269
orecchiette with beet leaves, tuna, and olives, 135–136
oregano, 118
and anchovy crust, baked swordfish with, 212–213
flower buds and grilled pork chops, linguine with, 118–119
garlic and anchovy sauce, spaghetti with, 127

oyster(s):
artichoke and rosemary sauce on lingue, grilled salmon with, 218–219
fried, perciatelli with fresh herb pesto and, 159–160
fried garlicky, linguine with, 161–162

P

pancetta, 80
chick-peas with ricotta sauce and, 254–255
fettuccine fresca with, 85
lasagnette with white onions and, 81
mezze ziti with prosciutto, pistachios, peas and, 88–89
and olive sauce, free-form lasagne with, 87–88
pork and cream sauce, linguine verde with, 114–115
and provolone crostini, 13
spaghetti with, 82–83
spaghetti with tomatoes and, 83–84
and tomato, 17
whole wheat spaghetti with, 80
panino, tomato, asparagus, and hearts of palm, 15
Parmesan (Parmigiano-Reggiano) cheese, 56–57
parsley, 43
and anchovy butter, 3
and anchovy butter, linguine with, 126
frittata, fluffy, 43
and tomatoes, panfried sandwich steaks with, 187